THE MOVIES OF

WOODY ALLEN

A Short, Neurotic QUIZ Book

David Wild

A Perigee Book

Perigee Books
are published by
The Putnam Publishing Group
200 Madison Avenue
New York, NY 10016

Typeset by Fisher Composition, Inc.

Library of Congress Cataloging-in-Publication Data

Wild, David, date.
    The movies of Woody Allen.

    Filmography: p. 133
    1. Allen, Woody—Miscellanea. I. Title.
PN2287.A53W55   1987   791.43'028'0924   86-25131
ISBN 0-399-51307-8

Book design by The Sarabande Press

Printed in the United States of America
1   2   3   4   5   6   7   8   9   10

7130719

Thanks to Paul for the gig, Melanie for the advice, Catherine for the video hookup, and Woody for the movies.

CONTENTS _____

INTRODUCTION

In one of *Annie Hall*'s more romantic moments, Annie and Alvy are walking arm-in-arm along the East River, with New York City's night skyline behind them. Alvy turns and asks Annie if she loves him. Missing just a beat, Annie admits that "Yeah," she does. When Annie returns the question, Alvy explains that "love" is far too weak a word to express his feelings. "I . . . I lerve you," he tells her, "You know I lo-ove you, I . . . loff you. There are two f's."

The Movies of Woody Allen: A Short, Neurotic Quiz Book is for those among us who "loff" the films of Woody Allen with two f's. Last winter, during my first pilgrimage to see *Hannah and Her Sisters*, I had a chance to spend three hours on line with a thousand or so such Woody-loffers. We were all waiting to buy tickets for the evening show, and as the temperature dipped into the low twenties, the group in front of mine decided to send one of their number in search of coffee. When the chosen one returned from his appointed caffeine task, a friend asked if he'd had any trouble finding someone who'd break a twenty dollar bill for such a small order. "No," the coffee-bearer told his friends, "but the first guy I went to told me to go forth and multiply . . . but not in those exact words."

What nearly brought a neurotic tear to my eye was not simply that this fellow had successfully paraphrased the punchline of one of Allen's old stand-up routines, but that all of his friends—some obviously not yet born when the joke was first cracked—caught the reference and had a laugh.

For such individuals, Woody Allen has taken on a peculiar sort of importance. As any true Manhattanite knows, the streets of New York City are prowled regularly by bands of Alvies in search of their own Annie Halls. Such Woody-philes (or in the most extreme cases, Woody-clones) are not without their scriptural defense. In *Manhattan,*Yale accuses Ike of acting like he's God. "Hey, I've gotta pattern myself after somebody," Ike says on his own behalf. If you're going to have a hero, you could do a lot worse than Woody Allen. Furthermore, you don't have to be a short, funny, balding, semi-intellectual Jewish male New Yorker in order to appreciate Allen's work. On the other hand, as someone's grandmother might point out, it couldn't hurt.

In the interest of fair play (not to mention legal self-protection) *The Movies of Woody Allen* deals almost exclusively with the man's work, rather than the closely guarded details of his personal life. The quiz covers every film Allen has written, directed, and/or appeared in through 1986's *Hannah and Her Sisters*. This is not to suggest for a moment that all films have been dealt with democratically. I doubt that you would enjoy answering 100 questions about *Don't Drink The Water* any more than I would enjoy the mirthless struggle to make them up. I have—in the interest of expediting matters—abbreviated the occasional title. If, for instance, you have trouble deducing that *Everything You*

Ever Wanted stands for *Everything You Ever Wanted to Know About Sex* (*But Were Afraid to Ask)*, then perhaps you should put this book down now, while you still can. I've also taken the liberty of blending the names of the performers in Allen's films with the names of the characters they play. For this I don't feel a bit guilty, since Allen started blurring the lines between these groups a long time ago. Perhaps most importantly, the reader should note that my use of the familiar "Woody" throughout the book is not meant to imply that Mr. Allen and I lunch together at Elaine's on a regular basis, but only that I feel a genuine warmth for the man's extraordinary work.

One final point: *The Movies of Woody Allen* is in no way meant as a trivia book. For the last few months, I've spent more hours than can be considered healthy or normal watching the man's movies, and take it from me, there's nothing trivial about them.

SCORING ———————

There are twelve quizzes in this book, each one made up of 50 multiple choice, matching, true-false, quote identification, and direct factual questions. The first 45 questions in each quiz are worth two points each. The last 5 are bonus questions worth four points each. These bonus questions are also known as the "eggs," so named in honor of the concluding joke of *Annie Hall*— the one about the man whose brother thinks he's a chicken. The man would like to help his brother overcome this "fowl" mood, but is reluctant to turn his sibling in to the loony bin because . . . he needs the eggs. Like that man, you need the "eggs."

If you score 90–110 points on a quiz, congratulations, you're a Woodman! Being a Woodman (or, of course, Woodwoman) is the highest honor that can be bestowed upon a living individual, particularly an individual living in the greater New York area.

If you score 70–90 points, you've won a Tony (as in Tony Roberts). Having received a Tony entitles you to hang out at length, or indeed ad nauseam, with any Woodman or Woodwoman who'll let you. (*Warning to those who live and die in L.A.*: as Allen's oeuvre plainly indicates, a Woodman who spends too much time in the California sun risks being demoted to Tony status.)

If you score 40–70 points, you're a Munk (in homage to Jonathan Munk who plays Alvy as a child in *Annie Hall*). To be a Munk is to be a neophyte with only partial, albeit intense, exposure to the work of the original Woodman. Many late-comers to the cult of Woody will end up as Munks.

If, by some cruel and usual act of God, you score 0–40 points, it's Dishonorable Menschen for you. Perhaps you thought you were picking up that brand new *Woody Hayes Quiz Book*? In any case, you've got your work cut out for you. Get the VCR, rent the movies, buy the soundtrack albums, put up the posters, and eat the breakfast cereal.

THE QUIZZES

QUIZ 1 _____

1. In *Take the Money and Run* (1969), what instrument does Virgil (Woody Allen) play in his high school marching band?
   (a) Jew's harp
   (b) zither
   (c) Moog synthesizer
   (d) cello

2. The original title for *Annie Hall* (1977) was *Anhedonia*. What does *anhedonia* mean?
   (a) the inability to kill lobsters
   (b) the inability to date women of one's faith
   (c) the inability to experience pleasure
   (d) the inability to live below 57th Street

3. In *Bananas* (1971), which soon-to-be-famous actor appears as a subway thug who beats up an old lady?
   (a) William Hurt
   (b) Sylvester Stallone
   (c) Danny DeVito
   (d) Wallace Shawn

4. What's the name of the imaginary game show in *Everything You Ever Wanted to Know About Sex* (1972)?
   (a) "Wheel of Lust"
   (b) "What's My Perversion?"
   (c) "Let's Form a Zygote!"
   (d) "The Nookie Connection"

5. In *Hannah and Her Sisters,* what unusual feature does Micky (Woody Allen) say his analyst has installed in his office?
   (a) a hot tub   (c) a cash register
   (b) a torture rack   (d) a salad bar

6. Which is *not* one of Broadway Danny Rose's (Woody Allen) motley acts?
   (a) a blind xylophone player
   (b) a parrot who sings "I Got to Be Me"
   (c) a break-dancing dermatologist
   (d) a skating penguin dressed as a rabbi

7. How does the *Rolling Stone* reporter describe sex with Alvy (Woody Allen) in *Annie Hall?*
   (a) "a Gonzo   (c) "Sixty seconds
       experience"   of fear and
                          loathing"
   (b) "Kafkaesque"   (d) "just like
                          Altamont"

8. In *Bananas,* Fielding (Woody Allen) orders 1000 sandwiches to go. What kind of sandwiches were they?
   (a) Fluffernutter
   (b) grilled cheese
   (c) lox and Spam
   (d) banana

9. What is the only film in which Woody's character marries Diane Keaton's character?

10. Woody plays a character named Victor Shakapopolis in two movies. One was *What's*

Woody at the opening of the stage production of Play It
Again, Sam, *1969*

New, Pussy Cat? (1965). What was the other?
(a) *Stardust Memories* (1980)
(b) *Bananas*
(c) *Everything You Ever Wanted to Know About Sex*
(d) *Victor/Victoria*

11. Woody's been visibly balding in all of his film appearances. True or False?

A CELLULOID SMORGASBORD: Match the food with its cinematic significance.

12. Grammy Hall's specialty

13. What Alvy and Tracy (Mariel Hemingway) eat in bed in *Manhattan* (1979)

14. Sonia's (Diane Keaton) chilling dessert in *Love and Death* (1975)

15. Danny Rose's Thanksgiving spread

16. The rebel's main course in *Bananas*

17. Annie's goyishe order in *Annie Hall*

(a) lobster

(b) pastrami on white with lettuce and tomato

(c) turkey TV dinners

(d) "dynamite" ham

(e) cole slaw for 1000

(f) sleet

18. A fiery entree in   (g) blinis
    Stardust Memories

19. The rebel's side   (h) chinese food
    order in *Bananas*

20. *Annie Hall*'s lively   (i) rabbit
    meal

21. Battle scene snacks   (j) lizard
    in *Love and Death*

22. In *Bananas*, the dictator makes a deal with
    what American organization for military rein-
    forcements?
    (a) the Central Intelligence Agency
    (b) the Federal Bureau of Investigation
    (c) the Daughters of the American
        Revolution
    (d) the United Jewish Appeal

23. What ex–*Saturday Night Live* personality
    plays a movie executive in *Stardust Memories*?
    (a) Don Pardo   (c) Laraine
                               Newman
    (b) Garrett Morris   (d) Samurai Studio
                               Head

24. In *Annie Hall*, Alvy claims to be one of the few
    males who suffers from _____.
    (a) penis envy   (c) the Cinderella
                               Syndrome
    (b) morning sickness   (d) temporary
                               water weight
                               gain

25. What rock group is seen performing in *What's Up, Tiger Lily?* (1966)?
    - (a) The Ultimate Spinach
    - (b) The Electric Prunes
    - (c) The Strawberry Alarm Clock
    - (d) The Lovin' Spoonful

26. In *Love and Death*, Boris (Woody Allen) hits Sonia repeatedly over the head with _____.
    - (a) a blintze
    - (b) a bottle
    - (c) a herring
    - (d) a peasant

27. How many years did Miles (Woody Allen) "sleep" through in *Sleeper* (1973)?
    - (a) 8½
    - (b) 714
    - (c) 200
    - (d) 2001

28. The first words in *Zelig* (1983) are spoken by writer Susan Sontag. True or False?

29. Woody's excuse for not committing suicide in *Hannah and Her Sisters* (1986) is that "My parents would have been devastated. I would have had to _____."
    - (a) stop sending them money
    - (b) keep going to dinner Sundays
    - (c) go back into therapy
    - (d) shoot them first

30. Complete Woody's thought in *Stardust Memories*: "To you I'm an atheist. To God, I'm _____."
    - (a) the loyal opposition
    - (c) just another short, balding Jewish guy

(b) a land-locked
   Hebrew

(d) an unsatisfied
   customer

31. In *Annie Hall,* who does Alvy pull out from behind a movie poster in order to shut up a pretentious jerk behind him on line for *The Sorrow and the Pity?*
    (a) Eugene Hasenfus
    (b) Arnold
       Schwarzenegger
    (c) Irving Howe
    (d) Marshall
       McLuhan

32. Having silenced the jerk, Woody faces the camera, and says, "_____."
    (a) Don't you wish you could get famous people to do cameos?
    (b) Talk about deus ex machina
    (c) Boy, if life were only like this
    (d) What the hell was he doing back there?

33. In *Sleeper,* when Miles and Luna (Diane Keaton) recreate a scene from *A Streetcar Named Desire,* who gets to play Blanche DuBois?

34. In *Love and Death,* an already dead Boris says that he doesn't believe that God is evil, only that he's _____.
    (a) a narcoleptic
    (b) an underachiever
    (c) an anti-Semite
    (d) thinning a bit
       on the top

35. *The Purple Rose of Cairo* (1985) takes place during _____.
    (a) the Depression
    (b) the building of the
       Suez Canal
    (c) the Renaissance
    (d) the Pleistocene
       age

36. In *Play It Again, Sam* (1972), an overconfident Woody goes to drop off one of his blind dates, and tells Tony Roberts and Diane Keaton, "If I'm not down in a hour, _____."
    (a) call in the cavalry
    (b) contact the authorities
    (c) sublet my apartment
    (d) light a candle for me

THE OEUVRE GROOVE: Identify the movie the following quotes come from.

37. "An eye for an eye, a tooth for a tooth, and a nose for a nose."

38. "You're a comedian. You want to do mankind a real service? Tell funnier jokes."

39. "I don't sell my work by the yard."

40. "I just met a wonderful man. He's fictional, but you can't have everything."

41. "Behind his black-rimmed glasses was the coiled sexual power of a jungle cat."

42. "Hey, Ralph! How much is a copy of *Orgasm*?"

43. "La De Dah."

44. "May I interject one notion at this juncture?"

45. On the soundtrack of what movie does Woody play clarinet with the Preservation Hall Jazz Band?
    (a) *Interiors* (1978)
    (b) *Sleeper*
    (c) *Zelig*
    (d) *Heavy Metal*

EGGS

46. For what film role did *The Purple Rose of Cairo* star Jeff Daniels first become known?

47. Where was Woody on the night of the 1977 Academy Awards presentation when *Annie Hall* won awards for Best Picture and Best Screenplay and Woody Allen won for Best Director?
    (a) at the ceremony with Diane Keaton
    (b) at the ceremony with Mariel Hemingway
    (c) at the ceremony with Tony Roberts
    (d) playing ragtime clarinet at Michael's Pub

48. Before *Annie Hall*, who was the last director whose film won all three of those same Oscars? For what film did he win them?

49. What two movies in which Woody appears have a question in the title?

50. Which two movies that Woody directed include the name of his character in the title?

ANSWERS

1. d
2. c
3. b
4. b
5. d
6. c
7. b
8. b

9. *Love and Death*
10. c
11. True
12. d
13. h
14. f
15. c
16. j
17. b
18. i
19. e
20. a
21. g
22. d
23. c
24. a
25. d
26. b
27. c
28. True
29. d
30. a
31. d
32. c
33. Miles
34. b
35. a
36. c
37. *Sleeper*
38. *Stardust Memories*
39. *Hannah and Her Sisters*
40. *The Purple Rose of Cairo*
41. *Manhattan*
42. *Bananas*
43. *Annie Hall*
44. *Broadway Danny Rose*
45. b
46. Debra Winger's husband in *Terms of Endearment*
47. d
48. Orson Welles for *Citizen Kane*
49. *What's New, Pussycat?* and *What's Up, Tiger Lily?*
50. *Zelig* and *Broadway Danny Rose*

QUIZ 2 _____

1. What songwriting team wrote the title theme to *What's New, Pussycat?*
   (a) Bacharach and David
   (b) Leiber and Stoller
   (c) Goffin and King
   (d) Leopold and Loeb

2. Who sang the title theme to *What's New, Pussycat?*
   (a) Engelbert Humperdinck
   (b) Gary Puckett and the Union Gap
   (c) Tom Jones
   (d) Mel Torme

THE WORKING MAN'S WOODY: Match the film with Woody's job in it.

3. talent agent

4. film director

5. Russian aristocrat/war hero

6. criminal

7. film magazine editor

(a) *Bananas*

(b) *Hannah and Her Sisters*

(c) *Broadway Danny Rose* (1984)

(d) *Sleeper*

(e) *Zelig*

8. luncheonette cashier/bookie

9. evil mastermind

10. dresser of strippers

11. products tester

12. TV producer

13. chameleon

14. co-owner of a health food store

15. accountant/inventor

16. TV writer

(f) *Stardust Memories*

(g) *A Midsummer Night's Sex Comedy* (1982)

(h) *Take the Money and Run*

(i) *Manhattan*

(j) *Play It Again, Sam*

(k) *The Front* (1976)

(l) *What's New, Pussycat?*

(m) *Love and Death*

(n) *Casino Royale* (1967)

17. In *Zelig,* what does representative of The Holy Family Christian Organization say about Leonard Zelig (Woody Allen)?
    (a) "Let he among us who is not a lizard cast the first stone."
    (b) "In the Lord's eyes, we're all chameleons."
    (c) "We're each and every one of us God's reptiles."
    (d) "I say let's lynch the little hebe."

18. In *Manhattan,* Ike (Woody Allen) says that he believes people should mate for life, like pigeons or _____.

(a) dentists   (c) dinosaurs
(b) Catholics   (d) politicians

19. At the end of *Manhattan*, Ike successfully converts his ex-wife back to heterosexuality. True or False?

20. What distinguished stage actor plays Leopold in *A Midsummer Night's Sex Comedy*?
    (a) Jason Robards   (c) José Ferrer
    (b) Hume Cronyn   (d) Barnard Hughes

21. Who appears in an unbilled cameo as Sandy's (Woody Allen) personal assistant in *Stardust Memories*?
    (a) Elaine May   (c) Candice Bergen
    (b) Louise Lasser   (d) Billy Crystal

22. In *Love and Death*, Boris says that he sees life as an enormous _____?
    (a) vibrating egg   (c) restaurant
    (b) joke   (d) wheat field

23. Woody's modest proposal in *Casino Royale*: "We'll run amuck, and if you get tired, we'll _____."
    (a) eat Chinese   (c) walk amuck
    (b) head for Elaine's   (d) destroy the world

24. The title of the sexual research text by one of Woody's characters in *Everything You Ever Wanted to Know About Sex* is:
    (a) *The Naked and the Pale*

(b) *Love and Death: A Comparative Approach*
(c) *Advanced Sexual Positions: How to Achieve Them Without Laughing*
(d) *The Sensuous Goy: A Vanishing Breed*

25. For his athletic role in *Don't Drink the Water* (1969), Jackie Gleason worked out for six months, and dropped down to 165 pounds. True or False?

26. What's the name of the adult education course Annie takes in *Annie Hall*?
(a) "Contemporary Crisis in Western Man"
(b) "Existential Motifs in Russian Literature"
(c) "Shellfish: A Cognitive Approach"
(d) "A Literary Overview: From *Beowulf* to *The Love Machine*"

27. What does Annie call her professor in the course?
(a) "Teach"   (c) "David"
(b) "Professor"   (d) "Mister Kotter"

28. In *Take the Money and Run,* Virgil tries to stab a woman who's blackmailing him. What weapon does he accidently use on her?
(a) a turkey drumstick   (c) a gerbil
(b) a tennis racket   (d) a gub

29. In *The Purple Rose of Cairo,* what historical figure is Gil Shepard anxious to play in the movies?

Diane Keaton with Woody in New York, 1970

(a) Fatty Arbuckle   (c) Charles Lindbergh

(b) John Wilkes Booth   (d) James Buchanan

30. Dr. Bernardo in *Everything You Ever Wanted to Know About Sex* claims to be the first scientist to explain the connection between excessive masturbation and entering politics. True or False?

31. In what city does *Love and Death*'s Village Idiots Convention take place?
   (a) Chevy Chase   (c) Reykjavík
   (b) Minsk   (d) Chernobyl

32. In *Annie Hall*, Annie tells Alvy that he's what her grandmother would call "a real _____."
   (a) mensch   (c) Jew
   (b) dirt bag   (d) ham

33. The film version of *Play It Again, Sam* is set in San Francisco. True or False?

34. Ed Koch has a cameo as a kosher pizza delivery man in *A Midsummer Night's Sex Comedy*. True or False?

35. In *Broadway Danny Rose*, Danny books soul shows at the Apollo Theater. True or False?

36. Sam Cooke's "Chain Gang" is played repeatedly on the soundtrack of *Take the Money and Run*. True or False?

37. Leonard Zelig's father was a Yiddish actor

who played Puck in an Orthodox version of *A Midsummer Night's Dream*. True or False?

38. In *Love and Death*, Boris's brother is bayonetted to death by a Polish conscientious objector. True or False?

39. The doctor who tells Micky he can't have children in *Hannah and Her Sisters* is played by Benno Schmidt. In real life, Schmidt is not a medical doctor, but the president of _____.
    - (a) The New York Mets
    - (b) Planned Parenthood
    - (c) Yale University
    - (d) Anhedoniacs Anonymous

40. In *Everything You Ever Wanted to Know About Sex*, the police estimate that the breast is about a 4000 _____ cup.
    - (a) B
    - (b) D
    - (c) M
    - (d) X

41. How does Woody dispose of the giant breast?
    - (a) he leads it off a cliff
    - (b) he traps it in a giant bra
    - (c) he excites it to death
    - (d) he breast-feeds until it begs for mercy

42. In *Hannah and Her Sisters*, Elliot (Michael Caine) expresses his love to Lee by giving her a book of poems by _____.
    - (a) Wordsworth
    - (b) Yeats
    - (c) Leonard Nimoy
    - (d) Cummings

43. In *Zelig*, what's the name of the 1935 movie

that Warner Brothers is supposed to have made of Leonard Zelig's life?

(a) *Love That Snake!*
(c) *The Changing Man*
(b) *That's Conformity*
(d) *Chameleon Daze*

44. Tom Baxter never finds the Purple Rose of Cairo. True or False?

45. In which movie does Woody commit the ultra-modern faux pas of sneezing away a friend's stash of cocaine?

(a) *Manhattan*
(c) *What's Up, John Zaccaro?*
(b) *Sleeper*
(d) *Annie Hall*

EGGS

46. In *Don't Drink the Water*, Ted Bessell plays Axel Magee, the bumbling son of an American ambassador. What's the television role for which Bessell is best known?

47. Name three Woody Allen movies that feature subtitles in English.

48. What playwright is Yale Pollack (Michael Murphy) writing a book about in *Manhattan*?

(a) Clifford Odets
(c) Arthur Miller
(b) Eugene O'Neill
(d) Neil Simon

49. Frederick's (Max von Sydow) proclamation in *Hannah and Her Sisters*: "If Jesus came back and saw what was going on in his name, he'd never stop _____."

(a) networking

(b) throwing up

(c) suing Pat Robertson

(d) doing the talk show circuit

50. At one point Woody's title for *What's Up, Tiger Lily?* was *Pow.* True or False?

ANSWERS

1. a
2. c
3. c
4. f
5. m
6. h
7. j
8. k
9. n
10. l
11. a
12. b
13. e
14. d
15. g
16. i
17. d
18. b
19. False
20. c
21. b
22. c
23. c
24. c
25. False
26. b
27. c
28. a
29. c

30. True
31. b
32. c
33. True
34. False
35. False
36. False
37. True
38. True
39. c
40. d
41. b
42. d
43. c
44. True
45. d
46. Don Hollinger, Ann Marie's boyfriend on *That Girl*
47. *What's Up, Tiger Lily?*, *Everything You Ever Wanted to Know About Sex*, and *Annie Hall*
48. b
49. b
50. True

QUIZ 3 _____

1. Which of the following come-on lines does Woody use on Diane Keaton in *Play It Again, Sam*?
   (a) "You lookin' for Mr. Goodbar?"
   (b) "So what's your Hebrew name?"
   (c) "You have the most eyes I've ever seen."
   (d) "You ought to be in pictures."

2. In *Everything You Ever Wanted to Know About Sex*, Woody plays all of the following except what?
   (a) a court jester   (c) an Italian stud
   (b) a sperm   (d) a vasectomy patient

3. In *Annie Hall*, where on Coney Island does Alvy say he grew up?
   (a) at the freak show   (c) next to the falafel stand
   (b) under the roller coaster   (d) in the house of mirrors

4. What concession does Alvy's father run at Coney Island?
   (a) the cotton kreplach stand   (c) the water slide
   (b) the Tilt-A-World   (d) the bumper cars

5. What does Tony Roberts's character do for a living in *A Midsummer Night's Sex Comedy*?
   (a) he's a tennis pro
   (b) he's a gigolo
   (c) he's a Shakespearean scholar
   (d) he's a physician

6. Much of *Manhattan* was actually shot on a sound stage in southern Florida. True or False?

7. Which of the following buildings is *not* seen in *Hannah and Her Sisters*?
   (a) Mount Sinai Hospital
   (b) Metropolitan Opera
   (c) Trump Tower
   (d) the Chrysler Building

THE WORLD AS HIS SUBURB: Sometimes Woody's world-view extends beyond the borders of Manhattan. Match the out-of-town spots with the movies in which they are featured.

8. Where Annie Hall grew up

9. *Bananas'* island in the sun

10. Where Tina (Mia Farrow) lives in *Broadway Danny Rose*

11. Where *Interiors'* watery conclusion occurs

(a) Southampton

(b) Russia

(c) Chippewa Falls, Wisconsin

(d) Vulgaria

12. *Don't Drink the Water* here   (e) San Marcos

13. The site of *A Midsummer Night's Sex Comedy*   (f) Paris

14. Where *Love and Death* takes place   (g) Upstate New York

15. The setting for *What's New, Pussycat?*   (h) New Jersey

16. Alvy and Annie Hall have their first meeting over what game?
(a) bocci ball   (c) Scruples
(b) badminton   (d) tennis

17. In *Love and Death*, Young Gregor's son was somehow older than Old Gregor. True or False?

18. During his first marriage to Allison, *Annie Hall*'s Alvy becomes so obsessed with a historical event that he uses it as an excuse to avoid sex. What's the event?
(a) the Dred Scott Decision   (c) defeat of Thomas Dewey
(b) the assassination of JFK   (d) the rape of the Sabine women

19. Allison is played by Carol Kane. For what television role did she first become known?
(a) Buddy on *Family*   (c) Simpka on *Taxi*
(b) Kitten on *Father Knows Best*   (d) Rosebud on *The Citizen Kane Show*

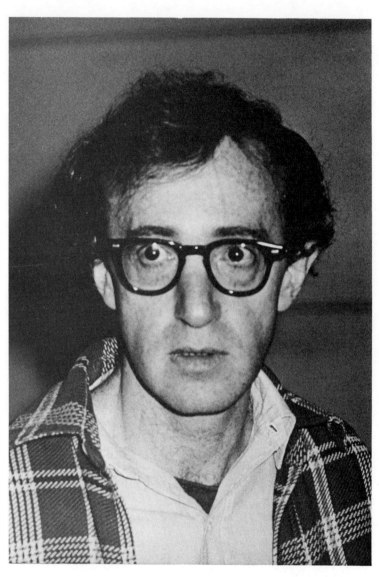

A harried Woody, 1977

20. In *Love and Death*, an old priest explains to young Boris that while Russian Jews have horns, German Jews have what?
    - (a) stripes
    - (b) feathers
    - (c) beaks
    - (d) trust funds

21. What question does young Boris ask the Grim Reaper about the afterlife?
    - (a) "Is there air conditioning?"
    - (b) "Are there girls?"
    - (c) "So, how's the corn beef?"
    - (d) "Is there a height requirement?"

22. Allan Felix (Woody Allen) says about a beautiful woman in *Play It Again, Sam*: "I'd trade my grandmother to the _____ for her."
    - (a) Celtics
    - (b) Arabs
    - (c) Russians
    - (d) Libyans

23. In *Stardust Memories*, Sandy goes to visit his sister, and sees her husband Sam riding an Exercycle. Sandy's sister tells Sandy that before Sam started riding, he had had two heart attacks. How many has he had since he started riding?
    - (a) none
    - (b) eight
    - (c) another two
    - (d) he can't remember

24. What distinguished actor plays Hannah's father in *Hannah and Her Sisters*?
    - (a) Don Ameche
    - (b) Lloyd Nolan
    - (c) Fred MacMurray
    - (d) Paul Hogan

25. Maureen O'Sullivan, who plays the mother of *Hannah and Her Sisters*, is the real-life mother of _____.
    (a) Gilbert O'Sullivan   (c) Mia Farrow
    (b) Michael Murphy   (d) Diane Keaton

26. Maureen O'Sullivan's best remembered screen role was _____.
    (a) Lou Gehrig's wife in *Pride of the Yankees*
    (b) Anne Frank in *The Diary of Anne Frank*
    (c) Doris in *Dancing Dough Boys*
    (d) Jane in the *Tarzan* movies

27. None of the characters in *Interiors* is an interior decorator. True or False?

28. Woody appears briefly in *Interiors* as the nutty, fun-loving judge who marries Arthur and Pearl. True or False?

29. In what movie is Diane Keaton seen eating raw meat?

30. In *Everything You Ever Wanted to Know About Sex*, Gene Wilder falls in love with _____.
    (a) Gilda Radner   (c) his own image
    (b) Woody Allen   (d) a sheep

31. In *Love and Death*, Sonia reports that Boris contemplated committing suicide by _____.
    (a) hanging himself
    (b) making a pass at the Brothers Karamazov
    (c) inhaling next to an Armenian
    (d) folk dancing

**FUTURE SHOCK: According to the scientists in
Sleeper, which of the following are good for you:**

32. wheat germ

33. cream pies

34. organic honey

35. smoking

36. deep fats

37. tiger's milk

38. How does Danny Rose describe his client who
    plays glasses?
    (a) the Issac Stern of tumblers
    (b) the Eddie Van Halen of Corning Ware
    (c) the Jascha Heifetz of her instrument
    (d) the Vladimir Horowitz of liquid containers

39. When the Countess in *Love and Death* tells
    Boris that he's the greatest lover she's ever
    had, he says what?
    (a) "Thanks, could you pass the lox?"
    (b) "Well, I practice a lot when I'm alone."
    (c) "There goes another novel."
    (d) "You weren't so bad yourself, my
        Lusciousness."

40. In *Annie Hall*, Alvy becomes convinced a rec-
    ord salesman is anti-Semitic when he tells
    Alvy there's a sale on _____.
    (a) Nazi sheet music   (c) Farrakhan
                                   posters
    (b) Kurt Waldheim's   (d) Wagner albums
        new rap record

41. In *Zelig*, Leonard says he first started becoming a chameleon when he dishonestly claimed to have read _____.
    - (a) Edmund Spenser's *The Faerie Queene*
    - (b) Herman Melville's *Moby Dick*
    - (c) the Talmud
    - (d) Woody Allen's *Side Effects*

42. In *Casino Royale*, Woody's character plots to eliminate every man in the world who is _____ than he is.
    - (a) funnier
    - (b) cuter
    - (c) taller
    - (d) more bald

43. In *Love and Death*, Boris confesses he can't eat any food that begins with the letter "f." What food does he give as an example?
    - (a) fettucini
    - (b) falafel
    - (c) fondue
    - (d) chicken

44. Jacqueline Bisset's character in *Casino Royale* is named Miss _____.
    - (a) Moneypenny
    - (b) Marble
    - (c) Lonelyhearts
    - (d) Goodthighs

45. Who plays Napoleon in *Love and Death*?
    - (a) J. R. R. Tolkien
    - (b) James Tolkan
    - (c) Alice B. Toklas
    - (d) James Toback

EGGS

46. What bridge do Mary and Ike sit together by in *Manhattan*?

47. In *Hannah and Her Sisters*, Micky considers converting to Christianity. What born-again

entertainer did Woody himself once work for as a joke writer?
(a) Pat Boone   (c) Amy Grant
(b) Little Richard   (d) Jerry Falwell

48. What bothers Micky about the philosophy of Nietzsche?
(a) He can't believe in any man whose name he can't spell.
(b) He'd hate to have to sit through The Ice Capades again.
(c) He'd have to listen to a German.
(d) He'd have to face the possibility of *CHIPS* reruns.

49. At the 1986 PEN Conference in New York City, who introduced Woody as "l'auteur des auteurs cinématiques"?
(a) Jerry Lewis   (c) Norman Mailer
(b) Andrew Sarris   (d) Philip Roth

50. The man who narrated *Take the Money and Run* performed the same duties for *Zelig*. True or False?

ANSWERS

1. c
2. d
3. b
4. d
5. d
6. False
7. c

8. c
9. e
10. h
11. a
12. d
13. g
14. b
15. f
16. d
17. True
18. b
19. c
20. a
21. b
22. b
23. c
24. b
25. c
26. d
27. False
28. False
29. *Sleeper*
30. d
31. c
32. Is not good for you
33. Is good for you
34. Is not good for you
35. Is good for you
36. Is good for you
37. Is not good for you
38. c
39. b
40. d
41. b
42. c
43. d
44. d
45. b
46. The 59th St. Bridge
47. a
48. b
49. c
50. False

QUIZ 4 _____

1. Who plays the sorcerer who makes Woody a love potion in *Everything You Ever Wanted to Know About Sex?*
   (a) Dr. Joyce Brothers (c) Billy Graham
   (b) Geoffrey Holder (d) Hugh Hefner

2. In *A Midsummer Night's Sex Comedy*, Andrew (Woody Allen) tries to explain away his relationship with Ariel by saying, "I went out with her once . . . had a couple of _____, that's it."
   (a) lobsters (c) weekends in the Catskills
   (b) games of hide the salami (d) children

3. In *Sleeper*, Woody wins a mock Miss America contest. What state does he have the honor to represent?
   (a) New Jersey (c) Alaska
   (b) New York (d) Missouri

4. In *Manhattan*, Ike quits his job to write a book. In reality, Allen's taken time off to publish a few books of his own writings. Which of the following is *not* one of his books?
   (a) *Side Effects* (c) *Getting Even*
   (b) *Expense Accounts* (d) *Without Feathers*

5. In what part of New York City is Arthur and Eve's apartment in *Interiors*?
   - (a) the upper East Side
   - (b) the upper West Side
   - (c) Hell's Kitchen
   - (d) Murray Hill

6. Ike says to Mary in *Manhattan*: "You look so beautiful. I can hardly keep my eyes on _____."
   - (a) Tracy
   - (b) Tina
   - (c) the meter
   - (d) the road

WOODY'S DATES: Match the picture with its year of release.

7. *What's New, Pussycat?* (a) 1969

8. *The Front* (b) 1979

9. *Sleeper* (c) 1985

10. *Manhattan* (d) 1965

11. *Take the Money and Run* (e) 1973

12. *The Purple Rose of Cairo* (f) 1976

13. Gil to Tom in *The Purple Rose of Cairo*: "You can't learn to be real. It's like learning to be a _____."
    - (a) rabbi
    - (b) caucasian
    - (c) Knicks fan
    - (d) midget

14. According to Alvy in *Annie Hall*, if you're in Freudian therapy and you commit suicide, you have to _____.
    (a) bring a note from your mother
    (b) be buried on a couch
    (c) pay for the sessions you miss
    (d) be buried near the Washington Monument

15. What's the leader of the American Federation called in *Sleeper*?
    (a) "The Big Cheese"
    (b) "Our Leader"
    (c) "Mister Mister"
    (d) "Top Gun"

16. In which movie does Woody threaten, "If she had made one more remark about Bergman, I would have knocked her other contact lens out"?
    (a) *Interiors*
    (b) *Manhattan*
    (c) *Stardust Memories*
    (d) *Take the Money and Run*

17. In *Manhattan*, Ike says he thinks something's wrong with him because he's never had a relationship with a woman that lasted longer than the one between _____.
    (a) Sacco and Vanzetti
    (b) Ticker, Evers and Chance
    (c) Hitler and Eva Braun
    (d) Roy Rogers and Dale Evans

18. In *Take the Money and Run*, a psychiatrist asks Virgil if he thinks sex is dirty. What's Virgil's reply?

(a) "It is if you do it right."

(b) "I'd certainly hope so."

(c) "I can only imagine."

(d) "Sex? What's sex?"

19. Name the movie in which Woody's character has three major love interests.

20. With what weapon is Alvy armed when he sets out to kill the spider in *Annie Hall*?
    (a) an Uzi rifle
    (b) a golf putter
    (c) a tennis racket
    (d) a kosher salami

21. In *Manhattan,* which of the following is *not* among the things that Ike lists as making his life worth living?
    (a) Flaubert's *Sentimental Education*
    (b) Walt Frazier's long shot
    (c) Groucho Marx
    (d) Swedish movies

22. When *Annie Hall* was first shown on NBC, Woody struck a deal in which the network could not remove from the soundtrack words it found obscene. True or False?

23. What's the significance of Ralph Rosenblum and Susan E. Morse in Woody's career?

24. Many consider the witnesses who discuss Leonard Zelig's life in *Zelig* a sly reference to similar characters in what movie?
    (a) *Witness*
    (b) *Judgment at Nuremburg*
    (c) *Reds*
    (d) *Pee-wee's Big Adventure*

THE NAME GAME: Match the first name of Woody's celluloid love interests with their correct last name.

25. *Play it Again, Sam's* Linda _____   (a) Vitale

26. *Manhattan's* Mary _____   (b) Fletcher

27. *The Front's* Florence _____   (c) Wilke

28. *Zelig's* Dr. Eudora _____   (d) Scholosser

29. *Broadway Danny Rose's* Tina _____   (e) Barrett

30. *A Midsummer Night's Sex Comedy's* Ariel _____   (f) Christie

31. *Sleeper's* Luna _____   (g) Weymouth

32. Woody appears in a cameo role in *Looking for Mr. Goodbar* as a psychopathic gay killer. True or False?

33. In the opening of *Annie Hall*, Woody tells a joke about two women at a Catskills resort. The first complains that the food is terrible. The second one says, "Yes, I know and _____."
    (a) the universe is expanding
    (b) the mah-jongg tiles have been tampered with

(c) the help are all Nazis

(d) the portions are so small

34. In *Manhattan*, what actress plays Ike's ex-wife who leaves him for another woman?
    (a) Louise Lasser   (c) Meryl Streep
    (b) Whoopi Goldberg   (d) Glenn Close

35. Howard Cosell's face can be seen in *Bananas, Sleeper* and *Broadway Danny Rose*. True or False?

36. *Hannah and Her Sisters* is the longest movie Woody Allen has ever directed. True or False?

37. *A Midsummer Night's Sex Comedy* takes place in the 20th century. True or False?

38. Marvin Hamlisch wrote the scores for both *Take the Money and Run* and *Bananas*. True or False?

39. Bella Abzug appears *sans* her trademark hat in *Manhattan*. True or False?

40. Throughout *Play It Again, Sam*, Tony Roberts's character is seen using a car phone. True or False?

41. In *Annie Hall*, Alvy asks an old man on the street how he and his wife keep their sex life exciting. The old man says their secret is that they use a large, vibrating _____?

(a) matzoh
(b) egg

(c) draydl
(d) sheep

42. Who plays Emma, the prostitute, in *The Purple Rose of Cairo*?
    (a) Dianne Wiest
    (b) Diana Ross
    (c) Diana Rigg
    (d) Dianne Brill

43. In *What's Up, Tiger Lily?*, the breasts of strippers are covered up by what words?
    (a) "Naughty Bits"
    (b) "Censored"
    (c) "Foreign Version"
    (d) "What Are You Looking At?"

44. What actor forgets his mantra in *Annie Hall*?
    (a) Jon Voight
    (b) Desi Arnaz
    (c) John Lithgow
    (d) Jeff Goldblum

45. In *Love and Death*, Sonia marries a man she does not love. What does he do for a living?
    (a) Cossack
    (b) caterer
    (c) marine biologist
    (d) herring merchant

EGGS

46. What's the name of the ex-costume designer for Woody who went on to direct the Mr. T. vehicle *D.C. Cab* and that Brat Pack classic *St. Elmo's Fire*?
    (a) John Hughes
    (b) Barry Levinson
    (c) Adrian Lye
    (d) Joel Schumacher

Woody and Diane Keaton at a Lincoln Center event, 1972

47. By the end of *Annie Hall*, Alvy's become a playwright. Which of the following is *not* a play Woody has written?
    (a) *God*
    (b) *Death Knocks*
    (c) *Scenes From a Seder*
    (d) *The Floating Lightbulb*

48. In Woody's original ending for *Take the Money and Run*, Virgil ends up bloodied and dead à la *Bonnie and Clyde*. True or False?

49. The original title for *Bananas* was _____.
    (a) *A Good Day for Gefilte Fish*
    (b) *El Weirdo*
    (c) *Revolution #1*
    (d) *What's Shaking, Salvador?*

50. After working with Woody, Louise Lasser went on to star in what television sitcom?
    (a) *Nanny and the Professor*
    (b) *Family Affair*
    (c) *What's Happening?*
    (d) *Mary Hartman, Mary Hartman*

ANSWERS

1. b
2. a
3. d
4. b
5. a
6. c
7. d

8. f
9. e
10. b
11. a
12. c
13. d
14. c
15. b
16. b
17. c
18. a
19. *Stardust Memories*
20. c
21. b
22. True
23. One or the other has edited all the films Woody's directed.
24. c
25. f
26. c
27. e
28. b
29. a
30. g
31. d
32. False
33. d
34. c
35. True
36. True
37. True
38. True
39. False
40. False
41. b
42. a
43. c
44. d
45. d
46. d
47. c
48. True
49. b
50. d

QUIZ 5 _____

1. In *Zelig*, what famous songwriter is said to have written the line "You're the tops. You're Leonard Zelig."
   (a) Marvin Hamlisch   (c) Paul Simon
   (b) Cole Porter   (d) Sammy Cahn

2. Why didn't the songwriter complete the song?
   (a) he died   (c) he got a better offer
   (b) he lost interest   (d) he couldn't find a word to rhyme with "Zelig"

3. In *Manhattan*, what's the name of Mary's ex-husband whom she calls an "oversexed, brilliant kind of animal"?
   (a) Thor   (c) Myron
   (b) Lance   (d) Jeremiah

4. In *Annie Hall*, Alvy says that he's heard that *Dissent* and *Commentary* have merged. What's the name of the resulting magazine?

5. Jack Lemmon plays Father Donnelly in *The Purple Rose of Cairo*. True or False?

6. In *Annie Hall*, Alvy meets his future ex-wife Allison (Carol Kane), and almost immediately reduces her to a cultural stereotype. Where does he guess she went to college?
   (a) Brandeis   (c) Barnard
   (b) Bates   (d) Bard

7. What artwork does Alvy think Allison's father would display in their home?
   (a) Currier & Ives prints   (c) Peter Max prints
   (b) Keith Haring posters   (d) Ben Shahn drawings

8. What's Allison's last name?
   (a) Nudnick   (c) Portchnick
   (b) Konigsberg   (d) Kramden

9. In which of the following films does Woody *not* appear?
   (a) *Zelig*   (c) *The Purple Rose of Cairo*
   (b) *What's Up, Tiger Lily?* (d) *What's New, Pussycat?*

10. In *Take the Money and Run*, Virgil shows his partners-in-crime a film of his plan for a big heist. What's the title of the short film he shows before the main feature?
    (a) *Trout Fishing in Quebec* (c) *Crime and Punishment*
    (b) *Hygiene and You*   (d) *The Bicycle Thief*

11. In *Zelig*, what well-known novelist says of Leonard Zelig, "He touched a nerve in people,

perhaps in a way they would prefer not to be touched."
(a) Saul Bellow
(b) Sinclair Lewis
(c) Brett Easton Ellis
(d) Stephen King

THE NAME GAME: Match the movies with Woody's last name in it.

12. *Annie Hall*'s Alvy   (a) Grushenko

13. *Take the Money and Run*'s Virgil   (b) Mellish

14. *The Front*'s Howard   (c) Davis

15. *Sleeper*'s Miles   (d) Starkwell

16. *Casino Royale*'s Little Jimmy   (e) Bates

17. *What's New, Pussycat*'s Victor   (f) Prince

18. *Bananas'* Fielding   (g) Singer

19. *Manhattan*'s Ike   (h) Felix

20. *Love and Death*'s Boris   (i) Monroe

21. *Stardust Memories'* Sandy   (j) Shakapopolis

22. *Play It Again, Sam*'s Allan   (k) Bond

23. In *Annie Hall*, Alvy's surprised by how much Annie pays for her nonstudio Manhattan

apartment. What's her monthly rent?

(a) $2000   (c) $600
(b) $400   (d) $800

24. Complete Mary's non sequitur in *Manhattan*: "I mean—really, I mean, I'm just from Philadelphia. You know, I mean we believe in _____."

(a) brotherly love (c) God
(b) elves   (d) cheese steaks

25. In *Sleeper*, Miles describes Howard Cosell as _____?

(a) a respected attorney (c) a professional wrestler
(b) a talented sportscaster (d) a form of punishment

26. Throughout *A Midsummer Night's Sex Comedy*, Maxwell (Tony Roberts) says that "_____ is the death of hope."

(a) marriage   (c) sex
(b) law school   (d) birth

27. In *The Front*, what does Howard Prince (Woody Allen) say was considered the biggest sin by his family?

(a) eating pork   (c) listening to Wagner
(b) voting Republican (d) buying retail

28. In which movie does Woody threaten to give Diane Keaton "a large and painful hickey"?

(a) *Annie Hall*   (c) *Manhattan*
(b) *Sleeper*   (d) *Interiors*

29. Officer Kojack—the evil Vulgarian official in *Don't Drink the Water*—is played by Michael Constantine. For what TV role is Constantine best remembered?
    (a) *The Jeffersons'* British neighbor
    (b) *Nanny and the Professor*'s professor
    (c) *Room 222's* principal
    (d) *F-Troop*'s Agarn

30. In *Everything You Ever Wanted to Know About Sex*, what does Tony Randall order the brain to think about during sex?
    (a) baseball players
    (b) Burt Reynolds
    (c) herring
    (d) George Bush

31. According to Miles in *Sleeper*, what did the Secret Service do every time Richard Nixon left the White House?
    (a) beat up Tricia
    (b) kick Checkers
    (c) ask out Pat
    (d) count the silverware

32. Howard Prince takes the Fifth at the end of *The Front*. True or False?

33. In what movie does Woody ask, "Did anyone read on the front page of the *Times* that matter is decaying?"
    (a) *Stardust Memories*
    (b) *Love and Death*
    (c) *Hannah and Her Sisters*
    (d) *Zelig*

34. Cecilia (Mia Farrow) never eats any popcorn in *The Purple Rose of Cairo*. True or False?

35. Woody is seen flying without the use of a plane in which two movies?

    (a) *Sleeper* and *Interiors*

    (b) *Zelig* and *Manhattan*

    (c) *Sleeper* and *Midsummer Night's Sex*

    (d) *Bananas* and *Stardust Memories*

36. In *Play It Again, Sam,* what does Woody say during lovemaking that suggests he's thinking about baseball?

    (a) "Say, Hey!"

    (b) "Slide!"

    (c) "Sign that kid up!"

    (d) "It's outta there!"

37. What's everyone fighting over in *What's Up, Tiger Lily?*

    (a) Kurosawa's first name

    (b) whether to go for sushi

    (c) heroin

    (d) a recipe for egg salad

38. Alvy's progress report on his therapy in *Annie Hall*: "Pretty soon when I lie down on the couch I won't have to _____."

    (a) fasten my seat belt

    (b) put on the straitjacket

    (c) use the plastic cover

    (d) wear the lobster bib

39. Which Woody Allen movie begins with the words, "Thank you. Thank you. If you ever overeat too much I got a great song"?

40. In *Sleeper,* Miles confesses that as a schoolboy he was regularly beaten up by whom?
    (a) Girl Scouts
    (b) Quakers
    (c) cantors
    (d) gym teachers

41. In *A Midsummer Night's Sex Comedy,* how many condoms does Maxwell say he's brought along for his romantic weekend in the country?
    (a) none
    (b) six
    (c) fifty
    (d) three hundred

42. According to Ike in *Manhattan,* what's the most overrated organ?
    (a) the pancreas
    (b) the colon
    (c) the Hammond
    (d) the brain

43. Which of the following is a machine used for sexual gratification in *Sleeper*?
    (a) the Love Lathe
    (b) the Orgasmatron
    (c) the Joy Stick
    (d) the Compact Disc

44. In *Bananas,* what does Esposito, San Marcos's guerilla leader, want as his country's national language?
    (a) Swedish
    (b) Yiddish
    (c) Pig Latin
    (d) Urdu

45. In *Annie Hall,* who in Alvy's family comes to the defense of their maid when she's caught stealing?
    (a) Alvy's father
    (b) Alvy's mother
    (c) Alvy
    (d) Joey Nichols

EGGS

46. A huge poster for what Humphrey Bogart movie hangs above Allan Felix's bed in *Play It Again, Sam?*
    (a) *The Big Sleep*
    (b) *Knock on Any Door*
    (c) *Across the Pacific*
    (d) *The Harder They Fall*

47. Name the two Woody Allen films shot in mock-documentary style.

48. Wallace Shawn, who plays Mary's ex-husband in *Manhattan,* is the son of _____.
    (a) comedian Dick Shawn
    (b) former *New Yorker* editor William Shawn
    (c) sex therapist Happy Shawn
    (d) actor Sean Connery

49. Joanna Gleason, who plays Tony Roberts's wife in *Hannah and Her Sisters*, is the real-life daughter of what game show host?
    (a) Monty Hall
    (b) Wink Martindale
    (c) Richard Dawson
    (d) Pat Sajak

50. Five years before Mel Brooks made *Blazing Saddles*, Woody wrote a screenplay for a Reformed Jewish western called *Chai Noon*. True or False?

ANSWERS

1. b
2. d
3. d

4. *Dysentery*
5. False
6. a
7. d
8. c
9. c
10. a
11. a
12. g
13. d
14. f
15. i
16. a
17. j
18. b
19. c
20. a
21. e
22. h
23. b
24. c
25. d
26. a
27. d
28. b
29. c
30. a
31. d
32. False
33. a
34. False
35. c
36. b
37. d
38. d
39. *Broadway Danny Rose*
40. b
41. d
42. d
43. b
44. a
45. a
46. c

47. *Take the Money and Run* and *Zelig*
48. b
49. a
50. False

QUIZ 6 _____

On his way home from Elaine's, 1978

1. Who plays the woman on the street in *Annie Hall* who explains to Alvy, "I'm very shallow and empty and I have no ideas and nothing interesting to say"?
   (a) Sally Field   (c) Joan Rivers
   (b) Farrah Fawcett   (d) Shelly Hack

2. In *Bananas*, Fielding orders 200 bacon, lettuce and tomato sandwiches to go. How many does he want on a roll?
   (a) 100   (c) 150
   (b) 1   (d) 0

3. According to *Sleeper*, what food chain will still be around in the 21st century?
   (a) Bagel Nosh   (c) Kentucky Fried Chicken
   (b) Burger King   (d) McDonald's

4. Which prominent film critic appears briefly in *Stardust Memories*?
   (a) Pauline Kael   (c) Judith Crist
   (b) Vincent Canby   (d) Leonard Maltin

5. Hannah's father about his wife in *Hannah and Her Sisters*: "She got drunker and drunker, and finally she became _____."
   (a) Joan Collins   (c) violent
   (b) sick to her stomach (d) Forster Brooks

6. In *Sleeper*, why did Miles go into the hospital in the first place?

(a) for a nose job
(b) for an ulcer operation

(c) for a vasectomy
(d) for the fun of it

7. Boris in *Love and Death*: "Some men don't think about sex at all. They become _____."
   (a) Republicans
   (b) irritable
   (c) husbands
   (d) podiatrists

8. Who plays Mia Farrow's sister in *The Purple Rose of Cairo*?
   (a) Linda Hunt
   (b) Sally Field
   (c) Stephanie Farrow
   (d) Barbara Hershey

HISTORICAL CHARACTERS: Which of the following is Leonard Zelig seen with in *Zelig*?

9. Babe Ruth

10. F. Scott Fitzgerald

11. Amelia Earhart

12. Joe McCarthy

13. Herbert Hoover

14. Fatty Arbuckle

15. Pope Pius XI

16. Tom Mix

17. Howard Cosell

18. Jack Dempsey

19. In *Love and Death*, when Boris tells Sonia, "Your skin is so beautiful," Sonia replies, "Yes, I know, _____."
    (a) I wear it all the time
    (b) I just got it dry cleaned
    (c) it's soft as a herring's behind
    (d) it covers my whole body

20. What is the only film besides *Casino Royale* in which Woody appears but did not write or co-write the script?

21. In *Manhattan*, what's Mary's ex-husband in town for when he and Mary bump into each other?
    (a) the Bicentennial   (c) the Whitney Biennial
    (b) the dog show   (d) a semantic symposium

22. In *Broadway Danny Rose*, Milton Berle agrees to come see Lou Canova's act at what establishment?
    (a) The Concord   (c) The Lone Star Cafe
    (b) The Waldorf   (d) Godfather's Pizza

23. What's the name of the underground leader Luna falls for in *Sleeper*?
    (a) Erno   (c) Sterno
    (b) Ernest   (d) Biff

24. Who plays Annie Hall's slightly suicidal brother Duane?

(a) Christopher Reeve   (c) Christopher
                              Lloyd

(b) Christopher   (c) Christopher Lee
    Walken

25. *A Midsummer Night's Sex Comedy* was released
    in the dead of winter. True or False?

26. *Everything You Ever Wanted to Know About Sex*
    is very loosely adapted from a book by whom?
    (a) Norman Mailer   (c) Dr. David
                               Reuben
    (b) Alex Hailey   (d) Dr. Hunter
                               Thompson

**THE FACES OF WOODY: In *Zelig*, Leonard Zelig is a
human chameleon. Which of the following does he
turn into?**

27. A Nazi

28. An Akita

29. A Chinese man

30. A flapper

31. A fat man

32. A Greek man

33. A professional lady golfer

34. An operatic clown

35. A flapper

36. A black man

37. A shrub

38. Which of the following actors stars in *Interiors*?
    (a) Daniel Stern   (c) Judd Nelson
    (b) Harrison Ford   (d) Sam Waterston

39. What's the name of the medley Lou Canova (Nick Apollo Forte) performs in *Broadway Danny Rose*?
    (a) "I Left My Heart With Tony Bennett"
    (b) "The Elusive Genius of Lionel Richie"
    (c) "Great Crooners of the Past Who Are Now Dead"
    (d) "A Meatball Medley"

40. What are the two movies Woody Allen directed but in which he does not appear?

41. Which of the following songs does not appear on the soundtrack of *Zelig*?
    (a) "You May Be Six   (c) "Chameleon
    People, But I Love   Days"
    You"
    (b) "Funky Lizard   (d) "Leonard the
    Weekend"   Lizard"

42. According to Tina, in *Broadway Danny Rose*, how did her husband die?

43. Which host's talk show does Lou Canova appear on in *Broadway Danny Rose*?
    (a) Dick Cavett's   (c) Larry King's
    (b) Tom Snyder's   (d) Joe Franklin's

44. While in Los Angeles, *Annie Hall*'s Alvy orders alfalfa sprouts and a plate of mashed yeast. True or False?

45. In his first scene in his first film, Woody is seen playing a game of _____.
    (a) Hüsker Dü
    (b) polo
    (c) chess
    (d) tennis

EGGS

46. Despite all his cinematic references to psychoanalysis, Woody himself has never been in therapy. True or False?

47. To what singer-actor was Mia Farrow once married?
    (a) Paul Simon
    (b) Bob Dylan
    (c) Frank Sinatra
    (d) Frankie Avalon

48. According to the editor of *Love and Death*, the Soviet Army assisted Woody in the filming of that movie. True or False?

49. *Broadway Danny Rose* takes place in the indefinite past. However, a 1983 movie title can clearly be seen at one point on a marquee. What movie is it?
    (a) *Zelig*
    (b) *Silkwood*
    (c) *Terms of Endearment*
    (d) *Halloween III*

50. In *Annie Hall*, when Alvy and Annie tell their respective psychiatrists how many times a week they sleep together, Alvy says it is "hardly ever," while Annie describes it as "constantly." How often is it?

(a) three times a week   (c) every three weeks

(b) quarterly   (d) once every three years

ANSWERS

1. d
2. b
3. d
4. c
5. a
6. b
7. d
8. c
9. Yes
10. Yes
11. No
12. No
13. Yes
14. No
15. Yes
16. Yes
17. No
18. Yes
19. d
20. *The Front*
21. d
22. b
23. a
24. b
25. False
26. c
27. Yes
28. No
29. Yes
30. No
31. Yes
32. Yes

33. No
34. Yes
35. No
36. Yes
37. No
38. d
39. c
40. *Interiors* and *The Purple Rose of Cairo*
41. b
42. He was shot in the eyes. Sorry, no partial credit for just saying he was shot.
43. d
44. True
45. c
46. False
47. c
48. True
49. d
50. a

QUIZ 7 ————————————

1. What politician is Alvy playing a benefit for when he meets his first wife in *Annie Hall*?
   - (a) Eugene McCarthy
   - (b) Joe McCarthy
   - (c) Norman Thomas
   - (d) Adlai Stevenson

2. Who plays singer Kitty Haines in *The Purple Rose of Cairo*?
   - (a) Rosemary Clooney
   - (b) Carole King
   - (c) Karen Ackers
   - (d) Kitty Kelly

3. In *Take the Money and Run*, why does Virgil's first big bank heist fail?
   - (a) bad planning
   - (b) bad karma
   - (c) bad weather
   - (d) bad penmanship

4. What New York City school does Tracy attend in *Manhattan*?
   - (a) The Albert Merrill School
   - (b) The Dalton School
   - (c) Barnard
   - (d) The Barbizon Beauty School

REWRITING HISTORY: Sleeper.

5. In *Sleeper*, who does Woody describe to future generations as having been the mayor of New York City?

    (a) Donald Trump
    (b) Bernhard Goetz
    (c) Bela Lugosi
    (d) himself

6. Whom does he say double-dated with God?
    (a) Charlie Manson
    (b) Senator Al D'Amato
    (c) Britt Ekland
    (d) Billy Graham

7. Whom does Woody describe as having been a famous French chef?
    (a) Idi Amin
    (b) Sam Cooke
    (c) Guy Lombardo
    (d) Charles de Gaulle

8. Whom does Woody say donated his ego to the Harvard Medical School?
    (a) Norman Mailer
    (b) George Hamilton
    (c) Johnny Carson
    (d) himself

9. In *Annie Hall*, Alvy says that the rest of the country thinks of New Yorkers as "left-wing, Communist, Jewish, homosexual _____."
    (a) investment bankers   (c) philanthropists
    (b) pornographers   (d) body builders

10. A dying gangster's last request in *What's Up, Tiger Lily?* is: "Don't use embalming fluid on me—I want to be stuffed with _____."

(a) crabmeat   (c) pork bellies
(b) chicken salad   (d) sushi

11. What actor plays Bogart in *Play It Again, Sam?*
    (a) Gary Busey   (c) Jerry Lacy
    (b) Sam Robards   (d) Wallace Shawn

12. What's the name of the secret governmental program that Miles and Luna try to stop in *Sleeper?*
    (a) The Aries Project   (c) The Harried Experiment
    (b) The Blues Project   (d) The Repression of the Masses

13. At the end of *The Purple Rose of Cairo,* Cecilia flies with Tom Baxter to Hollywood. True or False?

14. What's Annie Hall's nickname for her grandmother?
    (a) "Grandma" Hall   (c) "Grammy" Hall
    (b) "Jerry" Hall   (d) "Anthony Michael" Hall

WOODY'S WOMEN: Match the ladies with their roles.

15. His young love in *Manhattan*   (a) Susan Anspach

16. His real-life second wife   (b) Diane Keaton

17. His liberal love in *The Front*   (c) Lynn Redgrave

18. His anorexic girlfriend in *Stardust*

(d) Mariel Hemingway

19. His shrink/main squeeze in *Zelig*

(e) Louise Lasser

20. His wife in *Take the Money and Run*

(f) Andrea Marcovicci

21. His best friend's wife in *Play It Again, Sam*

(g) Mary Steenburgen

22. His ex-wife in *Play It Again, Sam*

(h) Janet Margolin

23. His royal love interest in *Everything You Ever Wanted to Know About Sex*

(i) Charlotte Rampling

24. His second wife in *Hannah and Her Sisters*

(j) Mia Farrow

25. His frigid wife in *A Midsummer Night's Sex Comedy*

(k) Dianne Wiest

26. In *Everything You Ever Wanted to Know About Sex,* what distinguished horror movie actor plays Dr. Bernardo, the crazed sex researcher?
    (a) Christopher Lee   (c) Lon Chaney, Jr.
    (b) Boris Karloff   (d) John Carradine

27. In *Annie Hall*, Alvy describes politicians as being "a notch under _____."
    (a) child molesters
    (b) studio executives
    (c) public relations people
    (d) ax murderers

28. Woody's excuse for not facing a firing squad in *Casino Royale* is that he has a low threshold of _____.
    (a) pain
    (b) panic
    (c) fear
    (d) death

29. In *The Purple Rose of Cairo*, which is not one of Gil Shepard's film credits?
    (a) *Dancing Dough Boys*
    (b) *The Depression II: First Crash*
    (c) *Honeymoon in Haiti*
    (d) *Broadway Baxters*

30. Which of the following celebrities does *not* appear on screen in *Broadway Danny Rose*?
    (a) Sammy Davis, Jr.
    (b) Big Bird
    (c) Geraldo Rivera
    (d) Milton Berle

31. Woody's request to Tony Roberts in *Hannah and Her Sisters* is: "The point here is that we need some _____."
    (a) ecstasy
    (b) women
    (c) money
    (d) sperm

32. In *Take the Money and Run*, how do Virgil's parents show their shame over their son's anti-social behavior?

(a) they kill
   themselves

(b) they kill Virgil

(c) they disguise
   themselves as
   Groucho Marx

(d) they convert to
   Catholicism

33. In *A Midsummer Night's Sex Comedy*, Woody's character says he's invented a machine capable of putting bones back into fish. True or False?

34. Which talk show host appears as himself in *Annie Hall*?
   (a) Tom Snyder
   (b) Dick Cavett
   (c) Jack Paar
   (d) Mike Douglas

35. How does Peter Sellers's character describe his wife in *What's New, Pussycat?*
   (a) "the lady in my
      life"
   (b) "the lady in the
      horns"
   (c) "the small
      building over
      there"
   (d) "the creature
      that ate
      Europe"

36. In *Annie Hall*, Alvy tells Rob that everything their parents said was good for them is actually bad for them, including sun, milk, red meat and _____.
   (a) guilt
   (b) the Democratic
      Party
   (c) sturgeon
   (d) college

37. In *Love and Death,* Boris claims to have been the men's freestyle _____ champion two years in a row.
    (a) fleeing
    (b) sweating
    (c) balding
    (d) kibbitzing

38. What did Broadway Danny Rose do before he became a manager?
    (a) he was a soldier of fortune
    (b) he was a herring merchant
    (c) he was a stand-up comedian
    (d) he was a free-lance florist

THE QUOTABLE WOODY: Match the quote with its source.

39. "Two Wongs Don't Make a Right."

40. "La De Dah."

41. "From my eye to God's ear."

42. "We're here to see the nose. We hear it's running."

43. "This is a madcapped, Manhattan weekend."

44. "I'm dating a girl wherein I can date her father."

(a) *The Purple Rose of Cairo*

(b) *Everything You Ever Wanted*

(c) *Sleeper*

(d) *Annie Hall*

(e) *What's Up, Tiger Lily?*

(f) *Manhattan*

Looking uptight, 1986

45. "I would never lay   (g) *Broadway Danny*
hands on the royal   *Rose*
tomatoes."

EGGS

46. Name two films in which Diane Keaton's character is a poet.

47. What distinguished stage actress plays Annie Hall's mother?
(a) Zoe Caldwell   (c) Jessica Tandy
(b) Maureen Stapleton   (d) Colleen Dewhurst

48. What's the name of the evil agency Woody's character works with in *Casino Royale*?
(a) KAOS   (d) LOX
(b) SMERSH   (d) HADASSAH

49. *Play It Again, Sam* opens with a scene from what Humphrey Bogart movie?

50. In a vignette removed from *Everything You Ever Wanted to Know About Sex* before its American release, Woody plays a spider who is devoured by fellow-spider Louise Lasser while making love. Allen also plays a gay scientist observing the spiders. The segment was entitled "What Makes a Man a Homosexual?" True or False?

ANSWERS

1. d
2. c
3. d
4. b
5. c
6. d
7. d
8. a
9. b
10. a
11. c
12. a
13. False
14. c
15. d
16. e
17. f
18. i
19. j
20. h
21. b
22. a
23. c
24. k
25. j
26. d
27. a
28. d
29. b
30. c
31. d
32. c
33. True
34. b
35. d
36. c
37. a
38. c
39. e

40. d
41. g
42. c
43. a
44. f
45. b
46. *Sleeper* and *Interiors*
47. d
48. b
49. *Casablanca*
50. True

QUIZ 8 _____

1. In *Manhattan*, what's the title of the short story about his mother that Ike says he'd like to expand into a novel?
   - (a) "The Castrating Zionist"
   - (b) "Mama, Mia"
   - (c) "Our Mothers, Our Shelves"
   - (d) "Mother, May I?"

2. Which of these questions does Virgil ask of his prison warden in *Take the Money and Run*?
   - (a) "What time you knock off work, honey?"
   - (b) "Excuse me, is there a side exit?"
   - (c) "Do you think it's right for a girl to pet on a first date?"
   - (d) "So, who's your caterer?"

3. After their split-up, Annie Hall calls Alvy in the middle of the night to come over and kill a _____ in her bathroom?
   - (a) cockroach
   - (b) burglar
   - (c) lobster
   - (d) spider

4. Under hypnosis in *Zelig*, Leonard tells Eudora all of the following *except*:
   - (a) her cooking is terrible.
   - (c) he misses Louise Lasser.

(b) he hates living in the country.

(d) he wants to sleep with her.

WOODY AND THE BOYS: Though Woody's known as a man who loves women, he always manages to find some work for representatives of the less gentle sex. Match the actor with his film appearance.

5. *Hannah*'s artful rock star

6. He forgets his mantra in *Annie Hall*

7. *The Front*'s blacklisted Heckie Greene

8. *Interior*'s father figure

9. *Everything*'s mad sex scientist

10. *Purple Rose*'s put-upon priest

11. He croons to one of *Hannah*'s sisters

12. *Annie Hall*'s mellow producer

13. A suburban gender-bender in *Everything*

(a) Paul Simon

(b) Lou Jacobi

(c) Milo O'Shea

(d) José Ferrer

(e) Michael Murphy

(f) Herschel Bernardi

(g) Tony Roberts

(h) E. G. Marshall

(i) Jeff Goldblum

14. *The Front*'s producer
    under pressure

(j) Tatsuya Mihashi

15. Keaton's poet-
    husband in *Interiors*

(k) Allen Garfield

16. *Midsummer*'s
    resident genius

(l) Daniel Stern

17. He's nailed to a
    cross in *Bananas*

(m) Bobby Short

18. He's *Tiger Lily*'s Phil
    Moscowitz

(n) John Carradine

19. He asks Woody to be
    The Front

(o) Zero Mostel

20. He's cheated on in
    Play It Again, Sam

(p) Richard Jordan

21. In *Interiors*, Diane Keaton's husband is played
    by actor Richard _____.
    (a) Gere   (c) Jordan
    (b) Roundtree   (d) Chamberlain

22. According to Miles in *Sleeper*: "Sex and Death.
    Two things that only happen once in a life-
    time. But at least after Death, you're not
    _____."
    (a) hungry   (c) sweaty
    (b) nauseous   (d) pregnant

23. In *Sleeper*, what organization does Miles de-
    scribe as "a group that helped criminals get
    guns so they could shoot citizens."
    (a) N.O.W.   (c) N.R.A.
    (b) P.O.W.   (d) E.P.C.O.T.

24. Alvy describes his first intimate encounter with Annie Hall as "the most fun I ever had without _____."
    (a) gagging
    (b) laughing
    (c) complaining
    (d) eating

25. The actress who plays Yale's wife in *Manhattan* is Ann _____.
    (a) DeSalvo
    (b) Jackson
    (c) Margret
    (d) Byrne

26. Which of the following men do not appear in *Purple Rose*?
    (a) Farley Granger
    (b) Van Johnson
    (c) John Wood
    (d) Milo O'Shea

27. What honor does the Carnegie Deli bestow on Broadway Danny Rose?
    (a) extra sour cream for his blintzes
    (b) lean corned beef for the price of regular
    (c) a sandwich named after him
    (d) a complimentary Bromo

28. In *Sleeper*, Luna says that men in the year 2073 are all impotent, with the exception of those of _____ descent.
    (a) Rumanian
    (b) Italian
    (c) Armenian
    (d) Japanese

29. In *Annie Hall*, who drives Alvy and Annie to the airport?
    (a) Annie's brother
    (b) Annie's father
    (c) Annie's grandmother
    (d) Annie's mother

30. At the end of *Manhattan,* where's Tracy going off to study?
    - (a) Paris's Folies Bergères
    - (b) London's Royal Academy of Music and Dramatic Arts
    - (c) L.A.'s Walt Disney Vocal Academy
    - (d) Rome's Opera Institute

31. Who plays the middle-aged transvestite in *Everything You Ever Wanted to Know About Sex?*
    - (a) Marty Allen
    - (b) Milton Berle
    - (c) Lou Jacobi
    - (d) Jack Gilford

32. What hit song was written for *Casino Royale?*
    - (a) "The Gambler"
    - (b) "Ramblin', Gamblin' Man"
    - (c) "Go All the Way"
    - (d) "The Look of Love"

33. In *Love and Death,* Sonia tells Boris that she's half angel, half whore. Which half does Boris say he wants?
    - (a) the half that's angel
    - (b) the half that's whore
    - (c) the half that drives
    - (d) the half that eats

34. The three main male characters in *A Midsummer Night's Sex Comedy* are all in love with one of the female characters. Which one?
    - (a) Ariel
    - (b) Adrian
    - (c) Dulcy
    - (d) the sheep

35. In *Annie Hall*, Alvy had a button that says "Impeach Reagan." True or False?

36. In *The Purple Rose of Cairo*, Tom Baxter has difficulty understanding the concept of God. With whom does he confuse the deity?
    (a) the projectionist
    (b) the men who wrote *The Purple Rose of Cairo*
    (c) President Hoover
    (d) the studio heads

37. In *A Midsummer Night's Sex Comedy*, what does Woody's character say when his wife suggests they make love on their kitchen table?
    (a) "Wait one second, I'll get the spatula."
    (b) "Watch out for that waffle iron!"
    (c) "No thanks, I've lost my appetite."
    (d) "We cannot have intercourse where we eat oatmeal."

38. In *Annie Hall*, Alvy says that he feels the world is divided into two things. What are they?
    (a) days the Knicks win and days they don't
    (b) those who are balding and those who aren't
    (c) the horrible and the miserable
    (d) love and death

39. In *Love and Death*, Boris describes death as being worse than _____.
    (a) the chicken at Treskie's Restaurant
    (b) puberty
    (c) Turgenev
    (d) life

40. Mia Farrow's first appearance in a Woody Allen film was in *Stardust Memories*. True or False?

41. In *Sleeper*, Miles and Monroe operate on what organ of the leader?
    (a) the liver   (c) the brain
    (b) the nose   (d) the heart

42. The name of the manager Lou Canova leaves Danny Rose for is Sid _____.
    (a) Vicious   (c) Konigsberg
    (b) Bernstein   (d) Bacharach

43. Which actress does not play either Hannah or one of her sisters?
    (a) Barbara Hershey   (c) Carrie Fisher
    (b) Dianne Wiest   (d) Mia Farrow

44. There are three sisters in the main families of both *Hannah and Her Sisters* and *Interiors*. True or False?

45. Woody approached Prince to write a theme song for *The Purple Rose of Cairo*. True or False?

EGGS

46. Name three movies in which Woody appears dressed as a rabbi.

47. Mariel Hemingway, one of Woody's notable love interests on film, is the granddaughter of Ernest Hemingway. True or False?

48. In *Play It Again, Sam,* the actress who plays Allen's blind date Julie is named Joy _____.
    (a) Stick
    (b) Berkowitz
    (c) Bang
    (d) Totheworld

49. In which one of Woody's movies do the two central characters' parents appear split-screen?

50. What publication not generally thought to be pornographic finds itself alongside *Screw* and *Orgasm* at a newsstand in *Bananas*?
    (a) *National Review*
    (b) *Limelights*
    (c) *The New Yorker*
    (d) *Commentary*

ANSWERS

1. a
2. c
3. d
4. c
5. l
6. i
7. o
8. h
9. n
10. c
11. m
12. a
13. b
14. f
15. p
16. d
17. k
18. j
19. e
20. g

21. c
22. b
23. c
24. b
25. d
26. a
27. c
28. b
29. a
30. b
31. c
32. d
33. d
34. a
35. True
36. b
37. d
38. c
39. a
40. False
41. b
42. d
43. c
44. True
45. False
46. *Take the Money and Run, Annie Hall* and *Zelig*
47. True
48. c
49. *Annie Hall*
50. a

QUIZ 9

1. In *Manhattan,* when Tracy suggests to Ike that they make love in a new, exotic way, he tells her to go get _____.
   - (a) her Twister game
   - (b) his golf clubs
   - (c) her Cuisinart
   - (d) his scuba equipment

2. Alvy describes Annie's grandmother as "a classic _____."
   - (a) beauty
   - (b) castrator
   - (c) Jew hater
   - (d) automobile

3. What's the name of Boris's brother who Sonia loves in *Love and Death*?
   - (a) Ivan
   - (b) Morris
   - (c) Alexander
   - (d) Eddie

THE COLLABORATIVE WOODY

4. He co-wrote *Take the Money and Run* and *Bananas.*
   - (a) Gordon Willis

5. He co-wrote *Annie Hall, Sleeper* and others.
   - (b) Marshall Brickman

Mia Farrow with Woody at New York City's annual Columbus Day Parade, 1984

6. He directed the photography from *Annie Hall* through *Purple Rose*.

(c) Carlo DiPalma

7. He directed the photography for *Hannah and Her Sisters*.

(d) Mickey Rose

8. In *Sleeper*, the name of what Big Band personality has become an adjective meaning better than "keen"?
   (a) "Ish Kibbible"   (c) "Whiteman"
   (b) "Satchmo"   (d) "Kugat"

9. Woody played the lead in *Play It Again, Sam* both in the film and on Broadway. True or False?

10. In *Manhattan*, a film director is about to make a movie about a man who is such a great lover that when he's had his way with a woman she dies from fulfillment. Who plays the film director?
    (a) Roman Polanski   (c) John Landis
    (b) Jeff Goldblum   (d) Michael O'Donoghue

11. In *Broadway Danny Rose*, Danny describes himself as a _____ Hebrew.
    (a) disco   (c) self-hating
    (b) land-locked   (d) split-level

WOODY KNOWS BEST: In which of the following movies is Woody's character seen with his child or children?

12. *Manhattan*

13. *Broadway Danny Rose*

14. *Sleeper*

15. *Take the Money and Run*

16. *Annie Hall*

17. *Hannah and Her Sisters*

18. Where does Micky take Holly for their unsuccessful first date in *Hannah and Her Sisters*?
    (a) The Carlyle
    (b) The Palladium
    (c) Mortimer's
    (d) *The Sorrow and the Pity*

19. Where does Holly take Micky on this same date?
    (a) Shea Stadium
    (b) CBGB's
    (c) professional wrestling
    (d) miniature golf

20. In *Annie Hall*, Annie tells her shrink about a dream in which _____ holds a pillow across her face so she can't breathe.
    (a) Frank Sinatra
    (b) a giant lobster
    (c) Art Garfunkel
    (d) her brother

21. In *Manhattan*, Mary claims that her dachshund is a _____ substitute.

(a) cat
(c) collie
(b) penis
(d) sugar

22. Boris's religious revelation in *Love and Death*: "And he shall dwell in the house of the Lord for six months, _____."
    (a) or until he finds a sublet
    (c) with an option to buy
    (b) or until the Lord notices
    (d) or longer if He has cable

23. In *Annie Hall*, Shelley Duvall plays a reporter for what magazine?
    (a) *Field and Stream*
    (c) *Commentary*
    (b) *Soldier of Fortune*
    (d) *Rolling Stone*

24. Mia Farrow's cruel husband Monk in *The Purple Rose of Cairo* is played by actor Danny _____.
    (a) Thomas
    (c) DeVito
    (b) Aiello
    (d) Aykroyd

25. What does Tina say she does for a living in *Broadway Danny Rose*?
    (a) independent record promotion
    (c) interior decoration
    (b) pinball machine maintenance
    (d) palm reading

26. The dictator in *Bananas* demands that each of his citizens present him with their weight in _____.
    (a) gold bullion
    (c) humus
    (b) bananas
    (d) horse manure

27. Where does Ike first meet Mary in *Manhattan*?
    - (a) Bagel Nosh
    - (b) The Museum of Modern Art
    - (c) The Castelli Gallery
    - (d) The Museum of Broadcasting

28. In *Annie Hall*, Alvy reports that the Army has him registered as 4P, which means in the event of war he's _____.
    - (a) booked on the first flight to Canada
    - (b) sent to the front first
    - (c) forced to join Bob Hope tours
    - (d) a hostage

29. Who plays Woody's sister in *Stardust Memories*?
    - (a) Annie De Salvo
    - (b) Gilda Radner
    - (c) Stephanie Farrow
    - (d) Marybeth Hurt

30. In *Hannah and Her Sisters*, Hannah and her mother have both played the same theatrical role. What role is it?
    - (a) Blanche DuBois in *A Streetcar Named Desire*
    - (b) Nora in *A Doll's House*
    - (c) Ophelia in *Hamlet*
    - (d) Mary Tyrone in *A Long Day's Journey into Night*

31. What real life game show host appears in *Everything You Ever Wanted to Know About Sex*?
    - (a) Jack Barry
    - (b) Wink Martindale
    - (c) Pat Sajak
    - (d) Richard Dawson

32. In *Annie Hall*, Woody's character is named Alvy, and Tony Roberts's is Rob. Both of them, however, keep calling each other by another name. What is that other name?
    (a) Ishmael   (c) Pepe
    (b) Max   (d) Kid

33. Most of the footage in *What's Up, Tiger Lily?* originally appeared in a Japanese movie called *Kagi No Kagi.* True or False?

THE INS AND OUTS OF WOODY: Which of the following films does Woody appear in?

34. *Play It Again, Sam*

35. *Interiors*

36. *What's New, Pussycat?*

37. *Don't Drink the Water*

38. *Zelig*

39. *The Purple Rose of Cairo*

40. *Fanny and Alexander*

41. *Bananas*

42. Who says "I never hit you. I always warn you first"? In what movie does he/she say it?
    (a) Woody to Janet Margolin in *Take the Money and Run*
    (b) Charlotte Rampling to Woody in *Stardust Memories*

   (c) Mariel Hemingway to Diane Keaton in *Manhattan*

   (d) Danny Aiello to Mia Farrow in *The Purple Rose of Cairo*

43. In *Bananas*, a TV ad for New Testament Cigarettes includes what line?
   (a) "Jesus died so that we might smoke."
   (b) "So join the flock, and light up for the Lord."
   (c) "I smoke them. *He* smokes them."
   (d) "The Lord is my nic fit, I shall not quit."

44. According to Boris, what's worse than death?
   (a) those long Russian winters
   (b) Hungarian women
   (c) an evening with an insurance salesman
   (d) life

45. Portions of *Love and Death* were filmed in what city?
   (a) Lanchester, Pa.
   (b) Budapest, Hungary
   (c) Prague, Czechoslovakia
   (d) Oxford, England

EGGS

46. In one of his routines in *Annie Hall*, Alvy claims he was thrown out of N.Y.U. What had he done wrong?

47. Julie Kavner plays one of Woody's television co-workers in *Hannah and Her Sisters*. For what TV role is Kavner best known?

48. In *Manhattan,* Mary admits that she once slept with one of her college professors. What grade did she get in the course?

49. In *Take the Money and Run,* the narrator says that Virgil was born on December 1, 1935. What key figure in Woody Allen's career was born on that day?

50. According to Alvy in *Annie Hall,* what's the only cultural advantage of Los Angeles?

ANSWERS

1. d
2. c
3. a
4. d
5. b
6. a
7. c
8. d
9. True
10. d
11. b
12. Yes
13. No
14. No
15. Yes
16. No
17. Yes
18. a
19. b
20. a
21. b
22. c
23. d
24. b

25. c
26. d
27. c
28. d
29. a
30. b
31. a
32. b
33. True
34. In
35. Out
36. In
37. Out
38. In
39. Out
40. Out
41. In
42. d
43. c
44. c
45. b
46. He cheated on his metaphysics exam by looking within the soul of the boy next to him.
47. Brenda, the sister of Rhoda Morgenstern on *Rhoda*.
48. F
49. Woody Allen
50. You can make a right turn on a red light.

QUIZ 10 _____

1. At what New York City hospital does Woody get his CAT scan in *Hannah and Her Sisters*?
   - (a) Columbia Presbyterian
   - (b) St. Vincent's
   - (c) New York Hospital
   - (d) Mount Sinai

DID WOODY DO IT?: Which of the following movies did Woody direct?

2. *Annie Hall*

3. *The Front*

4. *Don't Drink the Water*

5. *Sleeper*

6. *A Midsummer Night's Sex Comedy*

7. *Love and Death*

8. *Casino Royale*

9. In *Annie Hall*, Alvy says that when he got thrown out of college, his mother locked herself in the bathroom and overdosed on what?
   - (a) pork
   - (b) shellfish
   - (c) brisket
   - (d) mah-jongg tiles

10. Which Woody Allen film announces that it features "a no star cast" in the opening credits?
    - (a) *The Purple Rose of Cairo*
    - (b) *What's Up, Tiger Lily?*
    - (c) *Zelig*
    - (d) *Interiors*

11. Who plays Boris as a boy in *Love and Death*?
    - (a) Alfred Lutter III
    - (b) Alfred E. Newman
    - (c) Alfred Brooks
    - (d) Mark Linn-Baker

12. What's the name of the catering company Dianne Wiest and Carrie Fisher's characters start in *Hannah and Her Sisters*?
    - (a) Meals on Wheels
    - (b) Underachievers Limited
    - (c) the Stanislavski Catering Co.
    - (d) Cooks on Coke

13. In *Manhattan*, Ike tells Tracy that her voice sounds like who?
    - (a) Frankie Valli during puberty
    - (b) the mouse in Tom and Jerry
    - (c) Brett in *The Sun Also Rises*
    - (d) Donald Duck

14. Alvy tells Annie Hall that if he has too much pot or alcohol he gets unbearably _____.
    - (a) short
    - (b) wonderful
    - (c) horny
    - (d) hungry

15. At the end of *What's Up, Tiger Lily?* one of the main characters believes he's a Pan Am jet. True or False?

16. A news break in *Bananas*: "Astronauts have landed safely on the Moon and erected the first _____."

   (a) all-Protestant cafeteria
   (b) lunar condos
   (c) anti-semitic space station
   (d) Howard Cosell fan club

IT'S A LIVING: Match the actor with his/her screen profession.

17. Max von Sydow in *Hannah and Her Sisters*

   (a) architect

18. Danny Stern in *Stardust Memories*

   (b) psychiatrist

19. Janet Margolin in *Take the Money and Run*

   (c) sperm

20. Michael Caine in *Hannah and Her Sisters*

   (d) nurse

21. Irving Metzman in *The Purple Rose of Cairo*

   (e) actress

22. Corbett Monica in *Broadway Danny Rose*

   (f) financial adviser to rock stars

23. Anthony Quayle in *Everything You Ever Wanted*

   (g) professor

24. Peter Sellers in   (h) classical musician
    What's New,
    Pussycat?

25. Tony Roberts in *A*   (i) actor
    Midsummer Night's
    Sex Comedy

26. Michael Murphy in   (j) movie theater
    Manhattan   manager

27. Kristen Griffith in   (k) comedian
    Interiors

28. Sam Waterston in   (l) king
    Hannah and Her
    Sisters

29. Julie Hagerty in *A*   (m) painter
    Midsummer Night's
    Sex Comedy

30. Robert Walden in   (n) doctor
    Everything You Ever
    Wanted

31. Annie Hall's old actor-boyfriend Jerry tells her
    that he wants to die by being torn apart by
    _____.
    (a) reformed rabbis   (c) wild animals
    (b) sarcastic pygmies (d) Tony Roberts

32. What's the name of the mock TV show fea-
    tured in a skit on the series that Ike quits in
    Manhattan?

(a) "Down With People"

(c) "Matchgame 1984"

(b) "Grand Central Station"

(d) "Human Beings, Wow"

SHADES OF WOODY: Which of the following films are black and white? Which are color? And which one is both?

33. *Take the Money and Run*

34. *Manhattan*

35. *Sleeper*

36. *The Front*

37. *The Purple Rose of Cairo*

38. *Zelig*

39. *Love and Death*

40. *Interiors*

41. *Stardust Memories*

42. *Hannah and Her Sisters*

43. In *Everything You Ever Wanted to Know About Sex*, a rabbi gets to live out his sexual fantasy of being tied up and whipped by a beautiful model who tells him, "You've been a naughty rabbi," while his wife sits at his feet and _____?

(a) break dances

(b) crosses herself

(c) eats pork

(d) burns his yarmulke

44. What drug is Sandy's girlfriend Dorrie on in *Stardust Memories*?
    (a) cocaine (c) heroin
    (b) lithium (d) formaldehyde

45. In what movie does Woody request, "Could someone possibly sneak downstairs and let me back in?"
    (a) *Love and Death* (c) *Hannah and Her Sisters*
    (b) *Take the Money and Run* (d) *Zelig*

EGGS

46. In what two Woody Allen movies are the following lyrics sung: "Rebels are we / Born to be free / Just like the fish in the sea"?

47. In *Love and Death*, Woody duels with Harold Gould. For what is Gould best known?
    (a) being the father of Elliot Gould (c) playing Valerie Harper's dad on *Rhoda*
    (b) serving as spokesman for Gould's mustard (d) playing Tevye in the *Fiddler on the Roof* sitcom

48. Jeff Daniels was not originally cast in the male lead of *The Purple Rose of Cairo*. What actor did he replace after filming had already begun?

(a) Tom Hanks   (c) Steve
Guttenberg

(b) Michael Keaton   (d) Don Ameche

49. Who says, "I'm on the verge of a madcap Manhattan weekend"?
    (a) Boris in *Love and Death*
    (b) Tom in *The Purple Rose of Cairo*
    (c) Mary in *Manhattan*
    (d) the breast in *Everything You Ever Wanted to Know About Sex*

50. In *Sleeper*, what does the headline read on *The New York Times* from 1990 which Miles finds?
    (a) "DEWEY WINS!"
    (b) "POPE'S WIFE GIVES BIRTH TO TWINS!"
    (c) "AMELIA EARHART FOUND!"
    (d) "REAGAN RE-ELECTED"

ANSWERS

1. b
2. Yes
3. No
4. No
5. Yes
6. Yes
7. Yes
8. No
9. d
10. b
11. a
12. c
13. b

14. b
15. True
16. a
17. m
18. i
19. h
20. f
21. j
22. k
23. 1
24. b
25. n
26. g
27. e
28. a
29. d
30. c
31. c
32. d
33. Black and white
34. Black and white
35. Color
36. Color
37. Both. The movie within the movie is black and white, the rest is color.
38. Black and white
39. Color
40. Color
41. Black and white
42. Color
43. c
44. b
45. b
46. *Bananas* and *Sleeper*
47. c
48. d
49. b
50. b

QUIZ 11 _____

1. Where does Woody have his chat with a Hare Krishna follower in *Hannah and Her Sisters*?
   - (a) Kennedy Airport
   - (b) Washington Square Park
   - (c) Rockefeller Center
   - (d) Central Park

2. In *Annie Hall*, Annie tries to help Alvy stop smoking so much pot. True or False?

3. Complete this line from *The Purple Rose of Cairo*: "We should bring you to New York to meet the Countess. She loves anything in _____."
   - (a) a yarmulke
   - (b) horn-rimmed glasses
   - (c) a pith helmet
   - (d) the greater Metropolitan area

4. In *Manhattan*, Ike says that Mary deserves the _____ Emotional Maturity Award.
   - (a) Sylvia Plath
   - (b) Charles Manson
   - (c) Zelda Fitzgerald
   - (d) Phyllis Diller

5. In *Take the Money and Run*, Louise tells the interviewer, "The voting's unfair. It's who you know." What's she talking about?

(a) the Academy
Awards
(b) the Grammies

(c) the Presidential
Election
(d) the Ten Most
Wanted List

6. Woody's ambivalence toward rock music is well chronicled. In *Annie Hall*, what poor excuse does he give for missing a Bob Dylan concert?
   (a) he was expecting a death in the family
   (b) his raccoon had hepatitis
   (c) he couldn't find a thing to wear
   (d) he liked Dylan's earlier, funnier songs better

A SONG IN HIS HEART: Match the song with the movie in which it is played.

7. Gershwin's "Rhapsody in Blue"

(a) *Annie Hall*

8. The Lovin' Spoonful's "Gone Fishin'"

(b) *Everything You Ever Wanted*

9. "Do the Chameleon"

(c) *Interiors*

10. "Seems Like Old Times"

(d) *Play It Again, Sam*

11. "Hebrew School Rag"

(e) *Stardust Memories*

12. "Quiero la Noche"

(f) *What's Up, Tiger Lily?*

13. "Let's Misbehave"

(g) *Manhattan*

Looking chipper and stylish, 1981

14. Prokofiev's   (h) *Love and Death*
    "Alexander Nevsky"

15. Oscar Peterson's   (i) *Bananas*
    "Blues for Allan
    Felix"

16. "Wolverine Blues"   (j) *Zelig*

17. Which of the following is *not* a reason Woody's wife gives him for leaving in *Play It Again, Sam*?
    (a) she feels suffocated   (c) she can't stand the marriage
    (b) she doesn't dig him physically   (d) she likes his earlier funny movies better

18. When Ike and Mary get caught in a storm while walking through Central Park, where do they seek refuge?
    (a) The Hayden Planetarium   (c) The Metropolitan Museum of Art
    (b) The Hard Rock Cafe   (d) F.A.O. Schwartz

19. In what movie does Woody report that "I don't react well to mellow. I tend to ripen, then rot"?
    (a) *Manhattan*   (c) *Don't Drink the Water*
    (b) *Annie Hall*   (d) *Hannah and Her Sisters*

20. Danny Rose is constantly advising his clients to remember "The Three S's" which are "star, _____, strong."
    (a) sturgeon   (c) smile
    (b) stand   (d) satirize

21. In one segment of *Everything You Ever Wanted to Know About Sex*, Woody plays an Italian man whose wife can only enjoy making love _____.
    (a) in the Coliseum   (c) in public places
    (b) at the opera   (d) on pasta
                                primavera

22. Who takes a horse-drawn carriage ride through Central Park in *Manhattan*?
    (a) Ike and Mary   (c) Mary and Tracy
    (b) Ike and Tracy   (d) Tracy and Ike's
                                ex-wife

THE OEUVRE GROOVE: Identify the movie from which the following quotes come.

23. "Sir, you've been shot. When did you know it was all over?"

24. "Is he housebroken, or will he leave little batteries all over the floor?"

25. "But you just lay there—passive—like a lox."

26. "I'll let you have her at the old price . . . which is anything you want to give me."

27. "Not only is he a great agent, but he really gives great meeting."

28. In *Interiors,* with what color is Arthur's second wife, Pearl, associated?
    (a) black
    (b) white
    (c) red
    (d) paisley

29. Who plays Pearl?
    (a) Ruth Gordon
    (b) Anne Bancroft
    (c) Paula Prentiss
    (d) Maureen Stapleton

30. In *Interiors,* how does Joey angrily describe Pearl?
    (a) "She's a vulgarian!"
    (b) "She's a Bulgarian!"
    (c) "She's a Jewess!"
    (d) "She's a devil in a blue dress!"

31. What's the name of Mary's dog in *Manhattan*?
    (a) Martin Buber
    (b) Spot
    (c) Van Gogh
    (d) Waffles

32. According to Alvy, what's the size of the spider he's sent off to do battle with in Annie Hall's bathroom?
    (a) "as big as a Buick"
    (b) "the width of your Water Pic"
    (c) "the height of a hat rack"
    (d) "the length of a latke"

NAME THAT FILM

33. In which Woody makes his first film appearance.

34. In which Woody tells a congressional subcommittee to go fuck itself.

35. In which Woody serves hard time.

36. In which Woody's told he can't father a child.

37. In which Woody's beheaded.

38. In which Woody's shot by a fan.

39. In which Woody attempts a Russian folk dance.

40. In which Woody crosses the Hudson in a boat.

41. In which Woody's only seen lying on a couch.

42. In which Woody pretends he's a robot.

43. In which Woody gets hit with dozens of paternity suits.

44. In which Woody kisses a woman known as "The Detainer."

45. In which Woody is given a harmonica as a gift.

EGGS

46. What's the name of the animal Gene Wilder falls in love with in *Everything You Ever Wanted to Know About Sex*?
    (a) Wooly Bully   (c) Yvette
    (b) Babe   (d) Daisy

47. Name one feature film directed by Woody's collaborator Marshall Brickman.

48. In which film do Woody Allen and Diane Keaton appear as animated characters?

49. During the dictator's overthrow in *Bananas*, a baby carriage is seen falling down a set of stairs. What film is this a reference to?
    (a) *Rosemary's Baby*   (c) *Potemkin*
    (b) *The Bicycle Thief*   (b) *Small Change*

50. Which Bergman movie is Annie late to meet Alvy for in *Annie Hall*?
    (a) *Wild Strawberries*   (c) *The Seventh Seal*
    (b) *Face to Face*   (d) *Stewardess a Go-Go*

ANSWERS

1. d
2. False
3. c
4. c
5. d
6. b
7. g
8. f
9. j
10. a
11. e
12. i
13. b
14. h
15. d
16. c

17. d
18. a
19. b
20. c
21. c
22. b
23. *Bananas*
24. *Sleeper*
25. *Everything You Ever Wanted*
26. *Broadway Danny Rose*
27. *Annie Hall*
28. c
29. d
30. a
31. d
32. a
33. *What's New, Pussycat?*
34. *The Front*
35. *Take the Money and Run*
36. *Hannah and Her Sisters*
37. *Everything You Ever Wanted to Know About Sex*
38. *Stardust Memories*
39. *Love and Death*
40. *Broadway Danny Rose*
41. *What's Up, Tiger Lily?*
42. *Sleeper*
43. *Zelig*
44. *Casino Royale*
45. *Manhattan*
46. d
47. *Simon, Lovesick* or *The Manhattan Project*
48. *Annie Hall*
49. c
50. b

QUIZ 12 _____

1. In *Hannah and Her Sisters*, Micky says of his first date with Holly: "I had a great time tonight. It was like _____."
   - (a) the Bay of Pigs
   - (b) the Nuremberg Trials
   - (c) the Spanish Inquisition
   - (d) *Interiors*

2. Which of the following books does Alvy buy for Annie in *Annie Hall*?
   - (a) *The Naked and the Dead*
   - (b) *Death Wish*
   - (c) *Denial of Death*
   - (d) *My Life with The Grateful Dead*

3. The word "bananas" is never spoken in the movie *Bananas*. True or False?

4. Who plays Jackie Gleason's wife in *Don't Drink the Water*?
   - (a) Joyce Meadows
   - (b) Eileen Brennan
   - (c) Ann B. Davis
   - (d) Estelle Parsons

5. What historical figure does Boris try to assassinate in *Love and Death*?

Woody and Mia Farrow do their dueling penguins bit, 1986

(a) Lenin   (c) Napoleon
(b) Marx   (d) Dondi

6. In *Sleeper*, the government gives Miles a robotic _____ named Rex.
   (a) dog   (c) son
   (b) cat   (d) wife

7. In *Manhattan*, Ike tells Tracy that she's God's answer to what biblical figure?
   (a) Job   (c) Moses
   (b) Bathsheba   (d) Onan

8. At the end of *Casino Royale*, Woody's character is seen ascending to heaven. True or False?

Which of the following are characters' names in *What's Up, Tiger Lily?*

9. Terry Yaki

10. Suki Yaki

11. Benny Hannah

12. Phil Moscowitz

13. Mr. Chow

14. Shepard Wong

15. A song in *Zelig* contains the couplet, "Make a face that's like a lizard / and feel that down in your gizzard." True or False?

16. In *Interiors*, who plays Joey, the daughter "with no direction"?

(a) Amanda Plummer   (c) Diane Keaton
(b) Marybeth Hurt   (d) Debra Winger

17. How does Arthur, the father in *Interiors*, describe the world his wife Eve has created for their family?
    (a) "like a bad Bergman movie"
    (b) "like a Wasp nightmare"
    (c) "like an ice palace"
    (d) "like a rolling stone"

18. In *Hannah and Her Sisters*, what movie is Micky watching when he realizes that life is worth living?
    (a) *It's a Wonderful Life*
    (b) *Duck Soup*
    (c) *The Sorrow and the Pity*
    (d) *I Am Curious (Yellow)*

19. In *Annie Hall*, why does Alvy's mother bring her son to the doctor?
    (a) he refuses to eat
    (b) his hair begins thinning before his Bar Mitzvah
    (c) he's depressed because the universe is expanding
    (d) he's flunked metaphysics

20. In *Hannah and Her Sisters*, who does Lee (Barbara Hershey) end up marrying?
    (a) Frederick
    (b) Elliot
    (c) her dental assistant
    (d) her Columbia professor

THE OEUVRE GROOVE: Identify the movie from which the quotes come.

21. "My analyst warned me, but you were so beautiful that I—that I got a new analyst."

22. "I'm tired of marrying you every night. We never even get to the bedroom."

23. "It's amazing, Bash. From this he makes a living? I like a melodrama, a musical comedy with a plot."

24. "I've got a tumor in my head the size of a basketball!"

25. "Wheat. Fields and fields of wheat."

26. "I was in a black studies program. By now I could have been black."

27. "With most grievous dispatch, I will open the latch, and get to her snatch."

28. What's the name of the movie within *The Purple Rose of Cairo*?
    (a) *Steppin' Out*   (c) *Exteriors*
    (b) *Pennies from Hell* (d) *The Purple Rose of Cairo*

29. In *Manhattan*, Ike says that when it comes to romance he's the winner of _____.

(a) the August
Strindberg Award

(b) the Percy Shelley
Prize

(c) the Tennessee
Williams
Trophy

(d) the E. M.
Forster Cup

30. In *Annie Hall,* Alvy returns to his old grade school and hears what's become of some of his classmates. Which of the following is not one of the careers/fates mentioned?

(a) the president of
Pinkus Plumbing

(b) a tallis salesman

(c) a studio
executive

(d) a heroin addict

31. In *Broadway Danny Rose,* Danny and Tina are taken against their will to a warehouse. What's stored in the warehouse?

(a) wheat

(b) Lou Canova
records

(c) Macy's
Thanksgiving
Day Parade
floats

(d) beauty supplies

32. In *Sleeper,* what sort of business are the robots Ginsburg and Cohen in?

(a) theatrical
management

(b) catering

(c) ear, nose and
throat surgery

(d) custom tailoring

33. Toward the end of *The Purple Rose of Cairo,* Cecilia is forced to choose between two men. Whom does she choose?

(a) Gil Shepard

(b) Tom Baxter

(c) her husband Monk

(d) the popcorn sales boy

34. In his opening remarks to Annie Hall, what does Alvy claim is the worst that can be said of him?
    - (a) that he's self-obsessed
    - (b) that he's a self-hater
    - (c) that he's balding slightly on the top
    - (d) that he's a shark

35. The name of the movie theater in *The Purple Rose of Cairo* is the Thalia. True or False?

36. Who furnished Woody's clothes for *Stardust Memories*?
    - (a) Ralph Lauren
    - (b) Calvin Klein
    - (c) John Weitz
    - (d) Tom Waits

37. Which of the following songs is *not* part of Lou Canova's act in *Broadway Danny Rose*?
    - (a) "My Bambina"
    - (b) "Beer Belly Polka"
    - (c) "That's Amore"
    - (d) "Agita"

38. In *A Midsummer Night's Sex Comedy*, which female character does not have sex with Woody's character?
    - (a) Dulcy (Julie Hagerty)
    - (b) Ariel (Mia Farrow)
    - (c) Adrian (Mary Steenburgen)
    - (d) Fifi the Maid (Charo)

39. Which Woody Allen movie begins: "How I got into this predicament I'll never know. To be executed for a crime I never committed."
    (a) *Stardust Memories* (c) *A Midsummer Night's Sex Comedy*
    (b) *Love and Death* (d) *Sleeper*

40. At the end of *Bananas*, Howard Cosell is seen covering Fielding and Nancy's honeymoon for *Wide World of Sports*. True or False?

41. How does Alvy describe the pair of goons who approach him for autographs while he is waiting for Annie?
    (a) "the road company of *On the Waterfront*"
    (b) "teamsters on parade"
    (c) "a couple of classic Jew haters"
    (d) "two guys named Cheech"

42. In *The Purple Rose of Cairo*, Cecilia never gets to enter Tom Baxter's film world. True or False?

43. In *Hannah and Her Sisters*, which of the following does Micky *not* buy in his attempt to become a Catholic?
    (a) a Bible (c) a 700 Club membership
    (b) Wonder Bread (d) Hellmann's Mayonnaise

44. In *Take the Money and Run*, two groups of robbers try to hold up the same bank at the same time. True or False?

45. What character is seen having an out-of-body experience during lovemaking in *Annie Hall*?
    (a) Annie
    (b) Alvy
    (c) Joey Nichols
    (d) the lobster

EGGS

46. Which of Woody's movies has the longest title?

47. Which has the shortest title?

48. In what movie does Woody's character have a life-size photo of the My-Lai Massacre on his kitchen wall?

49. Throughout *Take the Money and Run,* people break something of Virgil's. What is it that they break?

50. At the end of *Manhattan,* Tony Roberts appears suddenly and gets into an argument with Michael Murphy over who's really Woody's best friend. True or False?

ANSWERS

1. b
2. c
3. False
4. d
5. c
6. a
7. a
8. False. He's descending into hell.

9. Yes
10. Yes
11. No
12. Yes
13. No
14. Yes
15. True
16. b
17. c
18. b
19. c
20. d
21. *Manhattan*
22. *The Purple Rose of Cairo*
23. *Stardust Memories*
24. *Hannah and Her Sisters*
25. *Love and Death*
26. *Bananas*
27. *Everything You Ever Wanted to Know About Sex*
28. d
29. a
30. c
31. c
32. d
33. a
34. c
35. False
36. a
37. b
38. a
39. b
40. True
41. d
42. False
43. c
44. True
45. a
46. *Everything You Ever Wanted to Know About Sex*
47. *Zelig*
48. *Stardust Memories*
49. His glasses
50. False

FILMOGRAPHY

What's New, Pussycat? (1965)
Directed by Clive Donner
Cast includes Peter Sellers, Peter O'Toole, Romy
Schneider, Woody Allen, Paula Prentiss, Capucine.

Woody's typically idiosyncratic screenplay does battle with the monster Hollywood and ends up getting
slayed. The considerable talents of Sellers, O'Toole and
the Woodman himself are generally wasted in this shrill
comedy that willed itself a smash by desperately trying
to please all the people all the time. The film—unlike
Ursula Andress who figures prominently in the concluding orgy sequence—has not aged particularly well.

What's Up, Tiger Lily? (1966)
Re-release directed by Woody Allen
Cast includes Tatsuya Mihashi, Mie Hama, Akiko
Wakabayashi, Tadao Nakamaru.

Woody takes a rather bizarre plunge into the world
of Japanese filmmaking and comes up with something
that would confuse even Kurosawa. He takes a dread-
ful-looking Japanese James Bond rip-off picture and
rewrites the dialogue into an hour and twenty minutes
of Jewish jokes. A wonderful soundtrack by The Lovin'
Spoonful and the occasional great line aren't enough
to sustain interest all the way through, and after the
first forty-five minutes all but the most dedicated fan
might want to take a sushi break.

Casino Royale (1967)
Directed by John Huston, Kenneth Hughes, Val Guest,
Robert Parrish

Cast includes Peter Sellers, David Niven, Ursula Andress, Orson Welles, Woody Allen.

"An unredeemingly moronic enterprise" is how Woody described this big-budget spoof of James Bond movies. Woody comes through to provide most of the few amusing moments in this film as Little Jimmy Bond, a meek, evil mastermind. Here we have conclusive proof that, in terms of directors, more is not always better.

Don't Drink the Water (1969)
Directed by Howard Morris
Cast includes Jackie Gleason, Ted Bessell, Estelle Parsons, Michael Constantine, Joan Delaney.

Not even the full-bodied presence of the great Jackie Gleason can save this remarkably unfunny adaptation of Woody's hit play, a comedy of errors about a nice Jewish family who get in big trouble when they go abroad. Director Morris, for reasons that soon become apparent, is best known as a feature performer on *Your Show of Shows*.

Take the Money and Run (1969)
Directed by Woody Allen
Cast includes Woody Allen, Janet Margolin, Marcel Hillaire, Jacqueline Hyde.

This winning comedy of crime and punishment holds up remarkably well. Allen's parody of the documentary form compares favorably to the later, more critically acclaimed *Zelig*. The basic concept—Woody as a Jewish Cool Hand Luke—provides plenty of wonderful material, particularly the scene in which his big heist fails due to bad penmanship.

Bananas (1971)
Directed by Woody Allen
Cast includes Woody Allen, Louise Lasser, Carlos Montalban.

Who says Woody's not a political filmmaker? This antic farce of Third World revolution isn't Woody at his most subtle, but it has more than its share of classic bits. Louise Lasser, Woody's second wife and future *Mary Hartman, Mary Hartman* star, is a wonderful foil, and the man himself is convincing as the apathetic products tester turned statesman.

Play It Again, Sam (1972)
Directed by Herbert Ross
Cast includes Woody Allen, Diane Keaton, Tony Roberts, Jerry Lacy.

Ross may have smoothed a few too many surfaces here but he still manages to convey the basic sweetness of Woody's play about a romantic misfit who falls for his wife's best friend. The wonderful timing between Woody, Diane Keaton, and Tony Roberts is a sign of good things to come in *Annie Hall*.

Everything You Ever Wanted to Know About Sex* (*But Were Afraid to Ask) (1972)
Directed by Woody Allen
Cast includes Woody Allen, Gene Wilder, Lou Jacobi, John Carradine, Lynn Redgrave, Tony Randall, Burt Reynolds.

A hit-and-miss affair of likeable perversity. The notion of a hundred-foot-tall breast, for instance, is more amusing in the conception than in the execution. Still, Woody's portrayal of a reluctant sperm in the final sketch is so convincing that it makes it worth sitting through a few questionable sheep jokes.

Sleeper (1973)
Directed by Woody Allen
Cast includes Woody Allen, Diane Keaton, John Beck, Mary Gregory.

Woody's at his most lovable as Miles Monroe, a nebishy health food store owner turned futuristic Rip van Winkle. In this inspired, gag-packed film, Woody finds a perfect vehicle to convey his love for the physical comedy of Charlie Chaplin, Buster Keaton, and Harold Lloyd. Woody's first screenplay collaboration with Marshall Brickman is possibly the only science fiction parody ever made with a Dixieland jazz soundtrack.

Love and Death (1975)
Directed by Woody Allen
Cast includes Woody Allen, Diane Keaton, Harold Gould, James Tolkan, Olga Georges-Picot.

Slapstick doesn't get any more literate than this. More than a brilliant genre parody of all things Russian, this is the film in which Woody begins to confront the big issues (see the title) that are the focus of many of his later films. He's also turning into a much more subtle director. His scattered references to Bergman, for instance, are ultimately a more fitting tribute to that bleak Swede than all of *Interiors*.

The Front (1976)
Directed by Martin Ritt
Cast includes Woody Allen, Zero Mostel, Herschel Bernardi, Andrea Marcovicci, Michael Murphy.

Woody takes a rare acting job in a film that takes a look at the lighter side of the McCarthy era. Zero Mostel, in one of his last film roles, gives a heartbreaking performance as a comedian who cannot live without work.

Annie Hall (1977)
Directed by Woody Allen
Cast includes Woody Allen, Diane Keaton, Tony Roberts, Paul Simon, Carol Kane, Shelley Duvall, Janet Margolin, Christopher Walken, Colleen Dewhurst.

Yes, it's as good as you remember it. For a commercial movie, *Annie Hall* unfolded in a terribly inventive nonlinear fashion. No matter, the film has its own internal logic. Diane Keaton delivers the finest performance of her career, as she manages to keep up with Woody, blow for blow, neurosis for neurosis. The supporting cast provides what seems like an endless series of inventive cameos. Woody establishes himself as a brilliant director and a romantic hero in one inspired stroke.

Interiors (1978)
Directed by Woody Allen
Cast includes Geraldine Page, E. G. Marshall, Diane Keaton, Marybeth Hurt, Kristin Griffith, Sam Waterston, Richard Jordan.

Woody does a decent Bergman imitation here, and

the performances are all impressive in a self-serious way. Do bring a sweater—this is as cold as cinema gets.

Manhattan (1979)
Directed by Woody Allen
Cast includes Woody Allen, Diane Keaton, Mariel Hemingway, Michael Murphy, Meryl Streep, Anne Byrne.

Critics greeted *Manhattan* as a definitive statement about life in the 1970s, particularly life as it was lived in New York City. The film's only flaw is that in examining the narcissism and smugness of those times, it occasionally engages in a little narcissism and smugness of its own. In any case, *Manhattan* is still one of the finest American films of the last few decades. And with the combination of George Gershwin's music and Gordon Willis's breathtaking black-and-white photography, it is also one of the most beautiful movies ever made.

Stardust Memories (1980)
Directed by Woody Allen
Cast includes Woody Allen, Charlotte Rampling, Marie-Christine Barrault, Jessica Harper, Tony Roberts.

A bleak but brilliant view of how lonely life can be at the top, even for a talented filmmaker with three enviable love interests. Attacked as being mean-spirited and self-indulgent, *Stardust Memories* is instead a brutally honest, self-critical piece of work that stands as one of Woody's major efforts.

A Midsummer Night's Sex Comedy (1982)
Directed by Woody Allen
Cast includes Woody Allen, Mia Farrow, Mary Steen-
burgen, Tony Roberts, José Ferrer, Julie Hagerty.

A leisurely paced examination of love and lust during one country weekend near the turn of the century *A
Midsummer Night's Sex Comedy* is a likeable curio. Gordon Willis's cinematography is overwhelmingly beautiful, making virtually every shot look like a painting.
But not many people laugh at paintings.

Zelig (1983)
Directed by Woody Allen
Cast includes Woody Allen, Mia Farrow, Ellen Gar-
rison, Mary Louise Wilson.

As a technical achievement, this meditation on conformity and celebrity is wildly impressive. The story of
Leonard Zelig—the human chameleon—is told dryly
in documentary form. Still, *Zelig* is held back from
complete success by its one-joke nature.

Broadway Danny Rose (1984)
Directed by Woody Allen
Cast includes Woody Allen, Mia Farrow, Nick Apollo
Forte, Corbett Monica, Howard Storm, Jackie Gayle,
Morty Gunty, Sandy Baron, Jack Rollins, Will Jordan.

Woody plays a schlemiel-saint in this long day's
journey into the Borscht Belt. Mia Farrow is wonderful, not to mention unrecognizable, as Tina, a tough
Italian lady and atrocious interior decorator from Fort
Lee, New Jersey. The film shows Woody making something of a return to his earlier slapstick comedy.

The Purple Rose of Cairo (1985)
Directed by Woody Allen
Cast includes Mia Farrow, Jeff Daniels, Danny Aiello, Ed Herrmann, John Wood, Deborah Rush, Van Johnson, Stephanie Farrow.

A somewhat surreal, bittersweet movie with some knowing things to say about the appeal of movies. Jeff Daniels is perfectly cast both as Tom Baxter, a second-tier leading man of 1930s Hollywood who steps out of one of his movies and as Gil Shepard, the self-obsessed actor who must track down his runaway characterization. Mia Farrow is just as good as a Depression-era wife victimized first by her husband and finally by her total trust in the magic of movies.

Hannah and Her Sisters (1986)
Directed by Woody Allen
Cast includes Woody Allen, Mia Farrow, Maureen O'Sullivan, Michael Caine, Barbara Hershey, Dianne Wiest, Max von Sydow, Lloyd Nolan, Carrie Fisher.

Woody confronts his interest in the interaction of three sisters with a much lighter touch than he exhibited in *Interiors*. He gives himself some dark, hilarious scenes as a hypochondriac looking systematically for the meaning of life. Who else could come up with a funny bit about a CAT scan? This marks a confident return to the ambitious filmmaking of his late '70s work.